Sustainability Starts at Home

HOW TO SAVE MONEY
WHILE SAVING THE PLANET

by Dawn Gifford

Small Footprint Family

Sustainability Starts at Home

How to Save Money While Saving the Planet

A compilation of essays from Small Footprint Family™, edited, updated, and revised for print.

Small Footprint Family's mission is to empower and inspire you with the tools and ideas you need to reduce your family's resource footprint so that you can save money, consume less, produce more, and live a more meaningful, healthy and sustainable life.

ISBN: 978-0692466469

This book is dedicated to my beloved daughter Naima, for whom I do everything I can so that she might inherit a world that is worth living in.

Praise for
Sustainability Starts at Home

"Your desk reference for an ethical 21st century lifestyle."

—Michael Hill, U.S. Forest Service

"As the wife of a LEED-certified Professional Building Analyst, and as a health blogger with an interest in green living, I'm pretty savvy when it comes to sustainability solutions in the home. But I was absolutely *floored* by how much I learned from this book! And more than a little shocked at how much more we could be doing to decrease our "footprint" and improve the sustainability of our lifestyle. You could easily save more than the cost of purchasing Sustainability Starts at Home in your first month of making these changes. **Everyone needs this!**"

—Emily Benfit, Butter Believer

"*Sustainability Starts at Home* not only explains WHY sustainability is so important, but shares HOW we can make positive changes that really make a difference. There are so many simple and innovative suggestions,

I had no trouble finding several that I can start implementing this week! This is a great read for anyone who wants to save time and get healthy while helping the planet at the same time."

—Elizabeth Walling, The Nourished Life

"*Sustainability Starts at Home* is great for newly aware people because it is simple to read and provides easy ways to be sustainable and save money. This book is also wonderful for people who have already been living green and want new ways to continue to minimize their footprint. There are countless tips and ideas on how to be more eco-friendly and Dawn really presents it in a way that anyone can understand.

I **love** this book – I absolutely and highly recommend it to each and every person!"

—Loriel Adams, Naturally Loriel

"*Sustainability Starts at Home* is a must-have resource for anyone who wants to save money while reducing their carbon footprint. Don't be intimidated, this book has shown me that it's easier than you think to start implementing small changes in your life now that will make a big difference...and most of them will even save you money. **This book pays for itself!**"

—Hannah Healy, Healy Eats Real

Disclaimer

Please know that although I do my very best to provide credible, defensible information that might make a difference in your life (like it has mine), this book reflects my personal research and experience, and nothing I write is in any way meant to constitute medical or financial advice.

Ultimately you are response-able for making your own informed decisions about your diet, lifestyle, finances, and health care. Google is your friend.

And, for heaven's sake, please don't print out part of this book and take it to your health care practitioner as "evidence" of anything!

Writers like me are SECONDARY sources of information, and no credible medical or dental professional will be swayed by anything other than PRIMARY sources of information—such as the peer-reviewed writings of other scientists and experts.

This is why I provide primary sources whenever possible, usually listed as links within the text and/or as resources at the end of the chapter.

Print *those* out and nail your doctor with *them*.

Contents

Saving Money on What You Buy

Introduction

Foreword

Are You Overwhelmed by "Going Green?"

You read the news about worsening air and water pollution, climate change, droughts and diminishing natural resources, and you worry if your family will have a healthy future. The problem seems so big and overwhelming. What can you do? Why bother?

You have the power and it starts right at home.

I have a seven year-old daughter who is the center of my world. I also see the proverbial "writing on the wall" about where we are headed environmentally, and I worry about my daughter's future.

But, I have wanted to throw up my hands at what seems like an unsurmountable, hopeless problem.

That's why I wrote this book.

But the good news is that change starts with each of us, right where we each live.

By making a series of small, doable changes, in aggregate, together we will make a big difference.

Are You Ready to Make A Difference?

In this book I'll share my extensive research into why today's environmental problems exist. I'll give you all the facts and data you need to understand the issues, then share simple, succinct action plans that you can easily implement right away.

You can start saving hundreds or even thousands of dollars a year, be empowered to greater self-sufficiency, reduce your carbon, water, energy and consumption footprints and have a tangible sense that you *are* making that difference.

What are You Waiting For?

- Discover how to save up to $200 a year simply by lowering your thermostat to this setting. *(Chapter 8)*

- Learn how to save 7,500 gallons of water and $140 in electricity costs every year, just by installing these inexpensive plumbing items. *(Chapter 12)*

- Get your home or business electricity from solar for less than the cost of your current utility bill—and lock in those prices for years to come. *(Chapter 11)*

- Follow these steps to buy all your organic produce and pasture-raised meat, dairy and eggs at wholesale cost *(Chapter 21)*

Sustainability Starts at Home will show you how to do all of this, plus give you hundreds more inspiring tips that will save you thousands of dollars a year—simply by making small adjustments to how you maintain your home and make your day-to-day purchases.

This book pays for itself (and then some) with the first tip you implement!

You Can Change the World, One Step at a Time!

I know that if you are reading these words, you are deeply concerned about the state of the world, and you worry about where we are headed if we keep doing things the same old way we always have been.

And, I know you care a lot about our beautiful earth and your family's future. You feel passionate about making a difference.

But it can often be challenging to know where to start.

And if you've already started and have gotten comfortable with things like composting or making your own non-toxic housecleaning solutions, you might want to know how to take your passion for green living and self-sufficiency to the next level.

This book has all the ideas, tips, facts and inspiration you need to help you live a simpler, more sustainable and frugal life—no matter what level of knowledge you are starting from.

Start with baby-steps; maybe take on implementing a chapter every month or so, and do as much as you can comfortably. You can even make a game out of trying some things that might be a little out of your current comfort zone to see how they work for you.

You **can** do it, and *every little effort does make a difference!*

Thank you for taking the first step.

— Dawn

I.

What is Sustainability?

Sustainability is, simply put, **the capacity to endure.**

It's about using what we need to live now, without jeopardizing the potential for people in the future to meet their needs, too.

If an activity is said to be sustainable, it should be able to continue *forever.*

When you start to think about what sustainability really means, you begin to glimpse just how deeply and systemically *everything needs to change.*

No longer can we deny the writing on the wall: Very little of what we do in modern life is capable of enduring. Very little of what we consume is produced sustainably.

Apocalypse Now?

Today, it is uncertain if our society has the capacity to endure— at least in a way that the nine billion people expected on Earth by 2050 will all be able to achieve a basic quality of life.

The planet's ecosystems are deteriorating and the climate is destabilizing fast. We are consuming so much, so quickly, that we are eating into our planetary capital, collectively consuming the renewable resources of 1.5 planets, according to the respected World Wildlife Fund / Global Footprint Network Living Planet Report [1].

And yet despite wasting about 40% of all our food, over a **billion** of our fellow humans go to bed hungry every night—both an unnecessary tragedy and a source of political unrest.

Meanwhile, our globalized world is more interconnected and volatile than ever, making us all more vulnerable.

Everything from the food we eat to the clothes we wear is dripping in fossil fuels and other extracted, finite resources from different parts of the world.

We are no longer able to easily extract oil and gas, except at grave cost to our atmosphere, fresh water supplies, and climate. We are running out of phosphate and potash, which will make industrial agriculture impossible.

We are running out of fresh water.

We think nothing of wasting precious fresh air and water, good topsoil and vast tracts of forest on single-use items like plastic water bottles, disposable diapers and toilet paper.

The accumulation of "stuff" is in fact the foundation of our economy, and the foundation of our destruction.

A culture that truly values their grandchildren's future would not do such crazy things!

There are no magic numbers, only trade-offs. Any given area of land can sustain many more very low-consuming, poor people at bare subsistence than it can very high-consuming, rich people living like millionaires.

Better technology always helps, but basically, the richer we all become, the fewer of us the planet—or any country in it—can sustain. And the more of us there are, the lower our sustainable standard of living will be.

The choice is fewer who are richer, or more who are poorer.

A New Paradigm

Living sustainably means balancing our consumption, our technology choices and our population numbers in order to live within the means of our bioregions, and the planet.

It means maintaining a stable and healthy environment for both humanity and all the flora and fauna with which we live in symbiosis.

Sustainable business and governmental policies would ensure the global conversion to renewable energy and renewable or recycled material sources, while phasing out those policies with harmful side effects.

Massive effort is needed to minimize waste of energy, water, food and other commodities. In this

This book was written to help you add up your own personal "triple bottom line" in all that you do.

It seeks to empower and inspire you with the tools you need to reduce your family's resource footprint so that you can save money, consume less, produce more, and live a more meaningful, healthy and sustainable life.

The world is counting on all of us to do our part.

What will you do?

Notes

1.   Living Planet Report - http://wwf.panda.org/about_ our_earth/all_publications/living_planet_report/

2.

Radical Simplicity Can Save Us

Everywhere around us, things seem to be getting more and more complex. And it's not good for our health or for the planet.

Whether it's the 35 different choices in the *water aisle* at the grocery store, or the new *need* for "smartphones" to organize every detail of our totally overwhelmed lives, or the gazillion forms you have to fill out to pay for medical care or to maintain your farm's organic certification, we seem to be increasingly burdened as a society by overchoice, micromanagement, and unnecessarily convoluted bureaucracies.

When the continuous operation of a system relies on a long and complex chain of suppliers and resources, all running smoothly, that's pretty much a textbook example of an **unsustainable** system.

Put another way, the systems we take for granted to deliver everything from widescreen TVs to food and fresh water are significantly more vulnerable than we may think.

According to Keith Farnish, author of *Time's Up: An Uncivilized Solution to a Global Crisis*:

> "We have been sold **'The Complexity Myth'**: the idea that something is only good if it is a product of a complex set of processes, in order that it (or we) can be controlled.
>
> We are kept in check by this idea and do not question it because we have forgotten how to live simply; we have been brainwashed to love the world of the complex, and as a result we are prepared to defend the thing that is caus-

ing the collapse of the natural world, and our own basic humanity."

To put it bluntly, we've become so utterly dependent on highly complex machinery, bureaucratic social structures and Byzantine systems to provide for nearly every aspect of our living, that if a crisis happened (like extreme weather, diminishing groundwater, or running out of oil), we'd all be up the proverbial "Shit's Creek."

I mean, would *you* be prepared if you lost electricity or water to your home for more than a week?

In today's chaotic and rapidly changing world, it is becoming increasingly common for disasters to disrupt modern facilities for at least that long.

The alternative: **Radical Simplification**

Simplicity *is* Sustainability

From greater health to greater happiness, simplification has so many benefits that it would not be possible to list them all here in detail.

But here are four benefits that I think capture the essence of simplicity, and destroy the myth that complexity is a good or acceptable thing (Ex-

cerpted from Keith Farnish for CultureChange.
org):

Simplicity Requires Less Energy

"This is self-evident, for the fewer stages there are
in any process, the less energy will be consumed
overall. You could argue that heating a house with
a load of wood and a hole in the ceiling is more
energy-intensive than a combination gas boiler,
but—setting aside the difference between renewable versus non-renewable forms of energy—in
order to manufacture the combination gas boiler
in the first place requires a similar number of processes as to manufacture a television.

If you really want more efficient heating, building a rocket stove from a few aluminum cans or
sheets of metal is relatively far simpler. In addition, the more stages involved in anything, the less
accountability is possible, and thus the more opportunity for energy waste."

Simplicity is Connected

"Following on from the previous point, accountability isn't really about economics, it is about
knowledge. If I were to buy a cord of wood that

had originated from a forest far away, then it would have had to pass through a number of stages to get from the source to the user: the felling of the trees; the sawing and preparation of the timber; the movement to the port and subsequent transportation by sea and/or land to the point at which it is available to me, or at least the person who gets it to me.

Through these different stages I have progressively lost connection with the origin of the wood; I have no sight of the trees, I cannot feel the soil, I cannot smell the air where the tree once stood. *I do not care.* That is the way of the civilized.

Compare this to a person who cuts her own wood from a tree she felled, and uses it to build a shelter. In other words, people connected to their resources do not poop where they eat."

Simplicity is Stable

"Complex societies are inherently unstable, for they rely on a multitude of different stages and processes connected by an equally complex set of linkages, any one of which can be critical to the efficient operation of the system as a whole.

Bring down a major power line to a process-
ing plant, shut down a distribution computer, or
blockade a port, and the whole dependent system
may break down, particularly one that is already
under stress, as so many systems are in the "just-
in-time" economy.

In contrast, if you grow your own food, or ideally
are a member of a local community of growers,
then you may be vulnerable to seasonal aberra-
tions or pests, but so long as you do it right then
your food supply is safe, and not subject to the
hazards of complexity."

Simplicity is Democratic

"Complexity is used to enforce the systems of
control that the Culture of Empire uses to keep
us subjects of that culture. One man with a sword
can control perhaps half a dozen people without
swords; one man with an agenda and a military
establishment under his control can control entire
nations.

Within a cooperative society, a simple society
working on egalitarian principles, no one can wield
power without challenge. You have a say, as does
everyone, for there can be no ivory towers or im-

pregnable fortresses in the simple society—you need complexity to build them."

According to Farnish, the mindset that brought us the equation **"civilization = better living = mind-boggling complexity"** is flawed and should be reconsidered in a 21st-century world of diminishing resources.

Put another way, if "the end of the world as we know it" came tomorrow, who would fare better: the people in the world who are living in simple, cooperative, agrarian villages, or the people in the world living in modern, industrial cities?

· ·

"Any intelligent fool can make things bigger and more complex... It takes a touch of genius—and a lot of courage—to move in the opposite direction."
—Albert Einstein

Get Real Simple

There is no singular correct way to simplify our complex way of living. The challenge is to add a bit of radical simplicity and self-sufficiency to your life every chance you get. This means **putting as few steps between you and what you need to be as healthy and happy as possible.**

Here are a few ideas, a number of which will be expanded upon in this book:

- Plant an organic vegetable garden, or yardshare with a neighbor and harvest more together.

- Grow fruit or nut trees.

- Raise some backyard chickens.

- Get rid of your TV, and in its place, take up something useful like gardening, woodworking, homebrewing beer, beekeeping, quilting, etc.

- Do any of the above with children.

- Join or start a Transition Community.

- Cloth diaper. Use washable cloth towels instead of paper towels. Hang your clothes to dry outside.

- Install a composting toilet, solar system, wood stove, drill a well, etc. Get "off the grid" to the extent you can.

- Quit eating foods that come in cans, bags and boxes, even if they are organic.

- Buy what you need locally as often as possible, especially local food.

- Barter and share instead of buying whenever possible.

- Make your own house cleaners and toiletries. The internet (and this book) are full of recipes for everything from homemade dishwasher detergent to shampoo to mascara.

- Commit to walking or biking everywhere you can. Use public transportation and ridesharing. Make driving solo a last resort.

- Experiment with buying nothing new for a year—except food, toiletries, socks and underwear. You may buy second-hand or do swapping, when needed.

- Join or start a food co-op, buying club, CSA or a credit union (or all four!).

- Get involved in political issues that affect your natural resources. Dangerous corporate practices like fracking, tarsands mining, mountaintop removal, GMOs, and the like threaten our ability to survive for generations to come.

. . . .

"Unless we are prepared to once again embrace the simple, then we have no future as a species.. except, perhaps those few remaining people who still live simply." —Keith Farnish

Saving Money
Around Your Home

3.

Reduce, Reuse and Only Then Recycle

There is a reason that recycling comes last in the often-repeated maxim of "reduce, reuse, recycle."

That is where it should be: **A last resort.**

Recycling is what we do with something when we have exhausted all opportunities to redesign the product to be more durable, to reuse or repair it, or to simply do without it altogether.

As a last resort, recycling is better than a landfill or incineration for sure. *But we shouldn't believe for a second that recycling will turn things around environmentally.*

. . . .

"The Story of Stuff" is a brilliant, upbeat little movie to share with your family about how reducing consumption can make us all healthier and wealthier. To watch, go to http://storyofstuff.org/movies/story-of-stuff/.

Reduce

Reducing the amount of "stuff" we consume is the surest way to reduce waste and save both natural resources and money.

To reduce both your household bills and your impact on the environment, consider an experimental, 30-day family **"spend-fast"**.

A spend-fast is where, for a set period of time, you voluntarily spend money *only* on the things you need to *survive*, like basic groceries (no expensive treats), doctor visits and transportation, for example.

Things to eliminate during a spend-fast might include lattés, potato chips, books and magazines, new clothing or movie rentals—whatever you buy that goes above and beyond your basic needs.

After doing this for a month or even just a week, it can be very enlightening to see how much money you can save and just how little stuff you really need to be happy.

Spend-fasting might even be habit-forming!

Another amazing way to reduce your consumption is by sharing things with your friends and community.

To that end, there are several websites that allow you to share your books, CDs, tools, toys, etc. with your friends, or whatever circles you decide to create.

Here are a few of the better ones:

- **SwapTrees.com** - Share books, CDs, DVDs, etc.

- **Neighborgoods.net** - Set up local circles to share whatever you want: tools, kitchen appliances, sporting equipment, etc.

- **Swap.com** - Baby and kid stuff swapping

- **BooksFreeSwap.com** - Book swapping

- **Peaceloveswap.com** - Local swapping

Reuse

Reusing and re-purposing things (sometimes called upcycling) are time-worn tricks I learned from my grandmother.

After living through the Great Depression, my grandmother darned her socks again and again until she could no longer repair them—even long after she had the money to buy new ones.

She also used to take the mesh bags onions and potatoes come in and sew them into very effective scrubbing pads for washing dishes. All her vegetable scraps became compost and fertilizer for next season's garden, and all my grandfather's old t-shirts became cleaning rags.

Very little actual trash left my grandparents' house. Not only did reusing and re-purposing their things save them tons of money when money was tight, but it made them planet-friendly conservationists decades before environmentalism was on anyone's mind.

Next time you're thinking of throwing something away, consider how you might repair it or creatively reuse it instead of sending it to the landfill.

Can you use old, torn clothing as a cleaning rags instead of buying paper towels—saving both trees and energy? Can it be composted? Can it be used for an arts and crafts project? There's really no limit to how you can reuse the things that no longer serve their original purpose!

If you really just can't find a new use for something, you can always give it away to charity or a local thrift store, or you can **Freecycle** it.

Freecycling is when a person directly passes on— for free—an unwanted item to another person who needs that item.

From silverware to mobile homes, people world-wide are choosing to give things away and freecycle rather than discard.

The practice frees up space in landfills and cuts down on the need to manufacture new goods. It's amazing what you can find on FreeCycle.org, Yerdle.com or Buynothingproject.org! Check them out!

. . . .

To reduce both your household bills and your impact on the environment, consider an experimental, 30-day family "spend-fast". See the chapter on Spend-Fasting for more details!

Recycle

As a last resort, you can recycle glass, cardboard, paper, aluminum and many types of plastic at the recycling center in your town. Most U.S. cities have curbside pickup for these common recyclable items.

Many cities also have **e-cycling** events where you can bring your old computer and electronic equipment for proper recycling and disposal (They often contain dangerous heavy metals and shouldn't be just thrown away).

Most U.S. Post Offices also carry postage-paid envelopes specifically for mailing off and recycling your used MP3 players, PDAs, cellphones and other handheld electronics.

You can also recycle certain electronics for cash by visiting www.EcoATM.com.

Whether you reduce your consumption, reuse, re-purpose, or freecycle old items, with a little creativity, reducing your garbage footprint can be easy, rewarding, and fun!

4.

Reduce Your Trash Footprint

We have a trash problem. A big one.

Humans all over the world have thrown away so much stuff, that we are running out of places to put it.

There are no places you can go anymore where you won't find *tons* of our trash. From Antarctica to the top of Mount Everest, and even deep into the ocean, thousands of miles from land and thousands of feet deep, you'll find bits of plastic, metal, glass and other waste that won't biodegrade for thousands of years.

In essence, we've totally trashed the place. We've pooped where we eat. If we were our own house-guest, we'd throw ourselves out!

(Oh, wait...)

And if that wasn't bad enough, "first world" nations like the United States have started exporting our trash to developing countries for disposal, so we don't have to see or deal with it.

These countries have few regulations or environmental protections, so dumping all of our trash on them (usually to be burned and picked through by poor people) has very grave consequence to the environment *and the children living there.*

The True Cost of Trash

While we will always need to purchase things, and there is nothing wrong with a few special luxuries now and then, we've gone way beyond acceptable limits and into pure gluttony.

We are burning up precious resources manufacturing and throwing away single use items like K-cups[1], water bottles and diapers[2]. We buy things only to dispose of them the next season or as soon as the next model comes out, and this has grave cost to future generations.

We really have to do something about our catastrophic levels of waste. *Now.*

Sustainability starts at home.

Change starts with you.

Here are several ideas...

Reduce, Reuse and then Recycle

The best way to reduce our trash problem is to simply **consume less.** Much of what we buy in the developed world we don't really need. And since we are currently using up the resources that our grandchildren will need to live, it only makes sense that we drastically cut back on what we buy today.

The second-best approach to reducing trash is to reuse, repurpose, upcycle, give away or Freecycle[3] things when they can no longer serve their original purpose. Anything that we can give a second or third life to will reduce the burden of trash upon the globe.

Lastly, we can recycle many things and use their raw materials in new ways. Glass, many plastics, aluminum cans, cardboard, paper, and even electronics can be taken apart, melted down and made into new things.

Recycling is really a **last resort** though: Even when things do get recycled, in the vast majority of cases, recycling only kicks the can down the road one generation. At some point that item will still be trash that can't or won't (because it costs too much) be recycled again.

Here are some ways that we can avoid creating trash in the first place. If you pay for trash collection, this will potentially save you a ton of money, too.

37 Ways to Reduce Your Trash

1. **Do a 30-day spend-fast** (See Chapter 16) to learn where you are making unnecessary purchases.

2. **Don't buy beverages in cans or single serving bottles.** For health's sake, don't buy soda or juice at all!

3. **Never buy bottled water.**[4] If you don't have access to a good well or spring, it is much better to get a good water filter and drink from the tap.

4. **Carry a glass, aluminum or steel reusable water bottle**. (Plastic will leach toxins.) This could be as simple as using a mason jar.

5. **Take a reusable travel mug to the coffee shop**, or make your coffee at home. Use a French press or coffee maker and avoid those single-serving packages used in Keurig-like machines, which are a *major* source of trash.[5] Try a reusable coffee filter in your coffee maker, too!

6. **Take your own reusable containers to takeout restaurants**. If you hand over the containers when you order and ask nicely, most restaurants will oblige you. For sustainable health, eat takeout less in general; most of it is full of GMOs, vegetable oils, MSG and other junk anyway.

7. **Take your lunch to school or work** and avoid takeout. Use a lunchbox and reusable snack bags. Not only is this healthier and cheaper,

but you get to keep more of your lunch break for yourself!

8. **Buy your milk in returnable, reusable glass bottles.** In many stores, you'll even get some money back for doing so!

9. **Buy your honey, pickled veggies, maple syrup, nut butters, and other wet foods in jars** you can reuse or return to the merchant.

10. **Return egg and berry cartons to the vendors** at the farmers' market for reuse.

11. **Bring your own reusable bags** when doing any kind of shopping.

12. **Shop for food from the bulk bins** and from farms, produce stands or the farmer's market, where food is unpackaged and fresh. Start a buying club (See Chapter 20) join a CSA (See Chapter 21) to reduce trash even further and make your food *very affordable*.

13. **Use lightweight cotton or nylon reusable bags** for both your produce and bulk items, too.

14. **Ditch the processed, packaged food altogether.** Make your own soup, yogurt, salad

dressing, ice-cream and other foods that come in cardboard, aluminum, and plastic packages. Batch cook on weekends with friends to make it easier. You'll save a ton of money, and eat *much, much* healthier this way too.

15. When you eat out, politely **ask your server to take away any paper or plastic napkins, placemats, straws, cups and single-serving containers,** if you can. Be sure to explain why and leave a nice tip for their trouble!

16. **Avoid buying anything that comes in wasteful single-serving packages,** like candy, gum, granola bars, popsicles, etc. Either make these from scratch or buy them bulk and put them in reusable snack bags.

17. **Cancel your magazine and newspaper subscriptions** and read them online or at the library.

18. **Buy e-books instead of paper books,** unless it is a reference book you will need if the power goes out. Use the library for books you don't want or need to own.

19. Do your best to **stop your junk mail.** (See Chapter 5.)

20. **Use both sides of a piece of paper** before re-cycling it or making it into upcycled crafts.

21. **Use old clothes and towels for rags** for cleaning around the house, instead of paper towels.

22. **Use cloth napkins and hand towels** in your kitchen.

23. **Don't use throwaway plastic razors and blade cartridges.** Consider an electric razor or waxing with cloth if you are a woman, or using an electric razor or a straight razor if you are a man.

24. **Consider non-disposable feminine-hygiene products such as a Diva Cup or Moon Cloth.** This is not only much better for the environment, it's *much, much* healthier for you too.

25. **Consider using family cloth[6] instead of toilet paper.** Really! It's softer, healthier and far less messy than you would think.

26. **Make your own non-toxic and effective toothpaste, deodorant, shampoo and even makeup.** There are tons of DIY recipes on the internet that will save you money and help you avoid toxic chemicals too.

27. **Use cloth diapers.**[7] They are super cute, frugal and *much* better for your baby's health, too.

28. **Carry a cloth handkerchief or napkin** for everything from blowing your nose to drying your hands to wrapping up a purchased doughnut.

29. **Make your own non-toxic household cleaners** to avoid all the chemicals and throwaway plastic bottles. (See Chapter 24.) Put your homemade cleaners in a recycled glass vinegar bottle with a repurposed spray nozzle.

30. **Use the plastic bags that other people's newspapers are delivered in** to pick up dog poop.

31. **Keep a worm bin or compost pile** to compost all your food scraps, leftovers, floor sweepings, and more. (See Chapter 14.)

32. **Avoid buying anything disposable.** Look for durable goods instead or borrow what you need. Paying a little more up front often means things will last much longer for you.

33. **Avoid buying anything in packaging when there is an unpackaged alternative** that is just as good (and count the money you save because that means buying mostly second hand).

You can also borrow things like tools, strollers and gardening equipment on Neighborgoods.[8]

34. **Give your old clothes to charities** or others who can use them.

35. **List items you no longer need on Freecycle or BuyNothing**[9], instead of throwing them away. (It's amazing what you can find on Freecycle or BuyNothing! You can sometimes even find motor homes!)

36. **Skip buying plastic garbage bags** and simply put your trash into the can itself. This will require you to wash the can from time to time, but if you are composting and recycling, it won't get too messy.

37. Make a game with your housemates or children to **see just how little trash you can create**, and how small you can make your garbage bag every week. Reducing our waste footprint can be a lot of fun!

Notes

1. http://www.theatlantic.com/technology/archive/2015/03/the-abominable-k-cup-coffee-pod-environment-problem/386501/

2. http://www.smallfootprintfamily.com/dangers-of-disposable-diapers

3. https://www.freecycle.org/

4. http://www.smallfootprintfamily.com/why-plastic-bottles-are-bad-for-the-environment

5. http://www.theatlantic.com/technology/archive/2015/03/the-abominable-k-cup-coffee-pod-environment-problem/386501/

6. http://www.thepolivkafamily.com/2013/06/no-more-toilet-paper-switching-to-cloth/

7. http://www.smallfootprintfamily.com/dangers-of-disposable-diapers

8. http://neighborgoods.net/

9. http://buynothingproject.org/find-a-group/

5.

Stop Your Junk Mail

Each American household receives almost 900 pieces of junk mail per year and wastes about 8 hours per year dealing with it. Here are some ways to get rid of this incredibly wasteful annoyance.

Why Junk Mail is Evil

Consider these scary statistics about junk mail:

The annual production and transport of junk mail consumes more energy than *2.8 million cars* idling 24-hours a day, seven days a week.

The amount of greenhouse gases produced in the yearly production, delivery and disposal of junk mail is equivalent to the output of 11 coal-fired power plants!

Annually, more than *100 million trees* are used to make junk mail—that's the equivalent of clearcutting the entire Rocky Mountain National Park every 4 months!

The Canadian Boreal forms part of the greater Boreal Forest, which stores more carbon than any other terrestrial ecosystem on earth. Despite this natural ability to protect us from the effects of climate change, the Canadian Boreal is being logged at a rate of 2 acres a minute[1], 24 hours a day to produce junk mail and other paper products.

Deforestation of Indonesia's tropical forests is responsible for 8% of global carbon emissions.[2] This destruction is largely driven by demand for pulp and paper for end uses like junk mail.

Logging contributes to Indonesia's status as the world's third largest emitter of CO_2 into the Earth's atmosphere, despite its relatively small size.

Approximately 44% of junk mail goes to landfills unopened, where it produces methane, a greenhouse gas 23 times more potent than carbon dioxide. State and local governments (and their citizens) spend hundreds of millions of dollars per year to collect and dispose of all the bulk mail that does not get recycled.

How to Stop Your Junk Mail

- **DirectMail.com** - free, quick way to get your name off commercial mailing lists.

- **CatalogChoice.org** - free service that'll get you on no-send lists to stop catalog spam.

- **OptOutPrescreen.com** - opt out of preapproved credit card and insurance offers online or by phone: 1-888-5-OPTOUT.

- **YellowPagesGoesGreen.org** - get your name off phonebook mailing lists.

- **EcoLogicalMail.org** - helps businesses stop mail addressed to former employees.

- **PaperKarma.com** - this awesome smartphone app lets you take photos of the unwanted mail you want to stop, then they automatically contact the mailer and remove you from their distribution list.

Some bulk mail items are sent to every resident on a postal route. These are addressed to "Resident," "Our Friends At," etc. Your postal carrier cannot, by law, determine what you consider junk mail. All "resident" mail must be delivered as addressed.

To stop this type of junk mail, you must contact individual mailers to have your address removed from their database. Look around on mailers for return addresses and phone numbers.

Here are quick links to some common ones.

- **America Online** - phone 1-800-605-4297.

- **Val-Pak coupons** - http://www.coxtarget.com/mailsuppression/s/DisplayMailSuppressionForm

- **Publisher's Clearinghouse** - phone 1-800-645-9242 or email service@pchmail.com with your full address and instructions to remove from mailing list.

- **American Family Sweepstakes** - phone 1-800-237-2400.

- **Redplum**, mailers of weekly sales circulars, can be reached at https://www.redplum.com/tools/redplum-postal-addremove.html. It will take a few weeks, but it will stop coming.

You should not receive mail if the mail or the accompanying card is not addressed to you, but your postal carrier may still deliver bulk sales circulars on "auto-pilot" after you have canceled them.

Remind your mail carrier politely that this junk is not addressed to you.

Junk E-mail May Be Worse

Once you've dealt with stopping junk mail in your mailbox, consider the other mail you get too. All of those junk e-mails that clutter up your inbox aren't just a massive annoyance but a colossal waste of energy.

According to a report released by computer security company McAfee, spammers generated a whopping **62 trillion junk e-mails** in 2009. (*Imagine what it is now!*)

What does that mean in terms of energy? Instead of sending messages asking for money or marketing Viagra, the electricity used sending the e-mails could have powered **2.4 million homes for a year or driven a car around the planet 1.6 times!**

That waste of energy is also polluting the environment. Almost everything powered by electricity also contributes to greenhouse gas emissions.

McAfee researchers say spam-related emissions for all e-mail users around the world in 2008 totaled 17 million metric tons of CO_2. That's .2 percent of the total global emissions—*just for spam!*

The report said that nearly 80 percent of the spam-related greenhouse gas emissions came from the energy burned by PC users viewing, deleting and searching for legitimate e-mail under mounds of junk.

About 80 to 90 percent of all e-mail is spam, but you can decrease your spam load by surfing the Net with a bit more care.

For example, anytime you participate in online discussions or post comments, make sure your user name is nothing like your e-mail address.

Also think twice before using the auto-complete feature on your browser because it may allow spammers to harvest personal information.

Some experts also advise changing your e-mail address yearly or using a temporary email address for all online shopping or opt-ins.

Lastly, using a good spam filter and other email security measures to make filtering and protecting your email easier is always a good practice.

Notes

1. http://www.nrcan.gc.ca/forests

2. http://www.forestethics.org/sites/forestethics. huang.radicaldesigns.org/files/dnmFactSheet.pdf

6.

The True Cost of Lighting

Several years ago, when compact fluorescent (CFL) light bulbs came onto the market, many environmentally conscious people were really happy.

And we were even happier when their prices came down and their warmth and quality improved greatly, because they really do save *a lot* of money, energy and natural resources.

But then we learned the ugly truth about CFLs:

Fluorescent light bulbs break sometimes, and when they do, they release mercury vapor into the air, and must be carefully removed and disposed of like toxic waste.[1]

You just can't put CFLs or other fluorescent bulbs in the trash—ever. *Yikes!*

If you break one, you need to rush your child out of the room until it can be ventilated of one of the **most toxic poisons known to humanity!**

But even more important than the tiny amount of mercury released by one broken bulb is the huge amount of mercury used in the *manufacture* of all CFLs.

This has far greater impact on the health of everyone, especially those who manufacture these bulbs.

That's why LED light bulbs are such Good News to people who want to save energy and money on their electric bills.

LED bulbs have many advantages over both incandescents *and* compact fluorescents:

• They use very, very little energy,

• last at least *10 years*,

- contain no mercury vapor,

- are tough and can be dropped or turned off and on repeatedly without damage,

- can operate in very cold or warm temperatures.

LED bulb prices will definitely give you a little sticker shock. However, at a lifetime cost of $86, compared to **$352 per bulb** for a standard incandescent, LEDs can clearly pay for themselves, *and* save you thousands of dollars in your home over time.

· ·

Replace your current bulbs with LEDs one at a time as they burn out, or when you can find them on sale. Amazon.com and Costco have some really good prices for LED bulbs, too.

And, just like with CFLs, the price is coming down quickly, and the efficiency and quality are improving at the same time.

American households spend up to 20% of their electricity costs on lighting. If every household switched to energy efficient light bulbs, we could prevent the release of 500 million tons of carbon dioxide per year!

Changing your light bulbs should be considered a very important part of your long-term strategy to save more money and reduce your family's resource footprint even further.

Even though it might look a bit bare, you can cut your energy consumption significantly and save up to $100 a year by removing half the bulbs from multi-bulb fixtures. Just make sure you can still see!

Given the ridiculous amount of fossil fuels burned every day so we can see in the dark, any improvement in lighting efficiency we make as a nation of families will also **decrease our dependence on foreign oil**, and **protect our air, water and natural resources at home**.

In fact, if every family and workplace replaced their standard incandescent bulbs with LEDs, we'd save **$3.9 billion per year,** and avoid emitting over **20 million metric tons** of pollution into the air![2]

Our nation could really use that kind of savings right now, don't you think?

Notes

1. How to properly dispose of a CFL - http://www.epa.gov/cfl/cflcleanup.html

2. http://www.lamps.com/resources/infographics/cost-of-lighting.html

7.

Slay the Energy Vampires in Your Home

Did you know that most of your appliances—cell phone chargers, computers, monitors, printers, televisions, DVD players, microwaves, coffee makers, and more—drain energy anytime they're plugged into a socket, regardless of whether they're turned on or off?

And not only that, but many electronics, like your plasma TV, don't actually go all the way off. Rather, they continue using "standby power" all day and night.

In fact, the average American home has **40 electronics** drawing power in off or standby mode, totaling **almost 10%** of residential electricity use.

The amount of standby power wasted varies among electronic equipment, but overall, the average household spends **$100 a year** on plugged-in devices that aren't being used directly.

· ·

Use a power strip for clusters of computer, electronic or kitchen products. That way you can switch everything to zero with one switch or even a remote control.

Nationwide, our idle gadgets and appliances suck up 100 billion kilowatt-hours of electricity—enough to power nearly 8.7 million homes—at a cost to consumers of about **$11 billion a year.**[1]

That's a ridiculous amount of money just thrown away on devices *we aren't even using*—money we all could really use right now!

And given that most of our electricity comes from expensive and polluting fossil fuels that are getting much harder and more dangerous to obtain, this is even more *outrageously* wasteful!

For the amount of energy the average home wastes on standby and phantom power, you might as well let the next three or four tanks of gas you buy pour out onto the cement.

In this light, reducing standby power consumption is practically a patriotic duty!

Here are some great ways to slay the "energy vampires" in your home:

- Get in the habit of unplugging all sleeping or not-in-use appliances. (Lamps are exempt.)

- Better yet, use a switchable power strip for clusters of computer, electronic or kitchen products. That way you can switch everything to zero with one switch or even a **remote control**. (The **Belkin Conserve** remote kits are made for this, enabling you to switch off plugs that are behind furniture using the remote.)

- When shopping, search for low standby products. (Asking a salesperson will probably be a waste of time.) Look for the ENERGY STAR label; these products have lower standby.

- Buy a low-cost watt-meter, measure all the devices in your home to see how much power they are *really* using, and take targeted action. You will be very surprised at what you discover and this exercise might even pay back the cost of the meter in savings. (The **Kill-a-Watt** is a great, affordable tool for this.)

· ·

When you put your hand on the plug or the appliance, if it's hot, it's using a lot of energy. If it's not hot, it's probably not using very much energy.

According to Bruce Nordman, an energy efficiency researcher at the Lawrence Berkeley National Laboratory, as a general rule, the bigger—and older—the device, the more power it sucks up while it's off.

So it's much more effective to unplug the decade-old TV in your guest bedroom than the phone charger that you bought last year.

These are the most power-hungry devices in your home, and should receive priority when deciding what to unplug or put on a powerstrip or Belkin Conserve-type unit:

Cable boxes: The *New York Times*[2] recently reported that cable boxes have an energy footprint far greater than their size would indicate. Indeed, the EPA estimates that cable box setups use about 500 kilowatt-hours per year—*as much electricity as your fridge.*

If you have more than one TV, you can request a multi-room box, which allows you to ditch all but one of your DVR devices. Put them on a power strip with your other entertainment devices, and turn them off when you aren't watching or recording.

Computers: According to the EPA, computers account for 2–3 percent of overall household and office energy use in the U.S. Sleep mode is good, but not nearly as good as unplugging entirely.

Laptops are more energy efficient, but **screensavers save nothing**. In fact, on a house by house level, a computer screensaver alone costs about $60 a year of electricity to maintain.

Shut off your computer and monitor when you leave work for the day. If your company backs up your computers at night on a network, just turn off your monitor.

Televisions: As a general rule of thumb, the bigger your TV, the more power it sucks, and the more diligent you should be about unplugging it.

Flat-screen TVs use about twice as much power as their smaller cathode-ray counterparts, and can *waste as much as $160 worth of energy annually when in standby mode.* That's a lot of money for an appliance you're not even using!

Audio/video: All those iPod docking stations, home theaters, DVD players, and Blu-ray players add up. Cluster these devices on a smart power strip when you can. Don't worry, many Energy Star-approved devices maintain their clock settings even when they're powered off.

Game consoles: People tend to leave game consoles on all the time. A recent Carnegie Mellon University study[3] estimated that power use by home game systems in the U.S. grew by 50 percent between 2007 and 2010 and now accounts for about *1 percent of total household energy use.*

Interestingly, the same study found that the Nintendo Wii uses significantly less energy than other popular systems (Microsoft Xbox and Sony Playstation).

Although many consoles now automatically switch to a power-saving idle mode after a period of inactivity, even "sleeping" games use some energy. Put it on a power strip and get your kid to shut it off entirely.

Digital picture frames: Because they use energy *all day long* just to sit there and show off pretty pictures, digital picture frames' energy use is significant. Find an Energy Star version or show off your best snapshots framed in good, old-fashioned wood and metal.

· ·

Unplug your cellphone and the charger once your phone is done charging. Once that light turns green, you are just wasting electricity.

Do Your Own Energy Audit

If you have older kids, a great homeschool or weekend learning activity is to use a **Kill-a-Watt** meter or similar device to measure the power usage of all the appliances in your home.

Together, you can then do an audit of your home energy use, and decide which appliances should be unplugged, put onto power strips or perhaps even be replaced.

Over time, you and your kids can take further energy saving measures in your home, and use your utility bill to gauge the results of your efforts. Then, do something fun as a family with the money you've saved!

When you slay the energy vampires in your home, you'll not only save lots of money, but also preserve clean air and water by reducing national fossil fuel usage.

And that's a win for everyone!

Notes

1. http://www.eia.gov/tools/faqs/faq.cfm?id=97&t=3

2. http://www.nytimes.com/2011/06/26/us/26cable.html?pagewanted=all

3. http://www.smallfootprintfamily.com/wp-content/uploads/vg_energy_savings_potential.pdf

8.

Seal Up the Leaks

Sealing air leaks around your house is the first step in a program to improve the energy efficiency of your home. The energy, time, and money you spend will pay for itself quickly—often in one winter!

If you live in an older house that has not been fully weatherized, somewhere between **20% and 50% of your heating bills can be attributed to air leakage alone!**

Air infiltrates into and out of your home through every hole and crack. About one-third of this air infiltrates through openings in your ceilings, walls, and floors.

One of the quickest ways you can save on your heating and cooling bill is to caulk, seal, and weatherstrip all seams, cracks, and openings to the outside.

Save up to $200 a year simply by lowering your thermostat from 70 degrees to 67 during the winter. You'll reduce your heating energy consumption by up to 5% for every degree below 70!

Sealing Home Air Leaks

First, test your home for air tightness. On a breezy day, carefully hold a lit incense stick or a smoke pencil next to your windows, doors, electrical boxes, plumbing fixtures, electrical outlets and switches, ceiling fixtures, baseboards, attic hatches, and other locations where there is a possible air path to the outside.

If the smoke stream travels horizontally, you have located an air leak that may need caulking, sealing, or weatherstripping.

Here are the main areas where most homes will need sealing:

- Caulk and weatherstrip baseboards, doors and windows that leak air.

- Caulk and seal air leaks where plumbing, ducting, or electrical wiring penetrates through walls, floors, ceilings, and soffits over cabinets.

- Install foam gaskets behind outlet and switch plates on walls.

- Look for dirty spots in your insulation, which often indicate holes where air leaks into and out of your house. You can seal the holes with low-expansion spray foam made for this purpose.

- Look for dirty spots on your ceiling paint and carpet, which may indicate air leaks at interior wall/ceiling joints and wall/floor joists. These joints can be caulked.

- Install storm windows over single-pane windows or replace them with more efficient windows, such as double-pane.

- Use an eco-friendly foam sealant around larger gaps around windows, baseboards, and other places where warm air may be leaking out.

- Kitchen exhaust fan covers can keep air from leaking in when the exhaust fan is not in use. The covers typically attach via magnets for ease of replacement.

- Replacing existing door bottoms and thresholds with ones that have pliable sealing gaskets is a great way to keep air from leaking out from underneath the doors.

- When the fireplace is not in use, keep the flue damper tightly closed. A chimney is designed specifically for smoke to escape, so until you close it, warm air escapes—24 hours a day!

- Fireplace flues are made from metal, and over time repeated heating and cooling can cause the metal to warp or break, creating a channel for hot or cold air loss.

  Inflatable chimney balloons are designed to fit beneath your fireplace flue during periods of non-use. They are made from several layers of durable plastic and can be removed easily and reused hundreds of times.

Should you forget to remove the balloon before making a fire, the balloon will automatically deflate within seconds of coming into contact with heat.

· ·

Install a programmable thermostat and use it to turn down your heating and cooling at night and while you are at work. By having the temperature in your house automatically regulated, you can reduce your energy use by up to 25% and save up to $300 on your utility bills.

A thorough job of leak sealing can cut your home's total air leakage by 33-46%—**reducing your heating bills up to 20%.** This winter, that could mean up to **$300 or more** in savings!

And the less you spend on heating and cooling, the less air and water pollution from coal plants we all must endure, and the more energy and natural resources we save for future generations, too!

9.

Upgrade Your Greedy Old Appliances

Many people believe that keeping old appliances is a form of recycling. But this is only half right.

True, you're not clogging up the landfills, but keeping the old stuff running isn't necessarily the greenest choice either.

Appliances account for about 17% of your home energy consumption, with refrigerators, and clothes washers and dryers at the top of the consumption list.

If you've got appliances that are more than 10 to 15 years old, they are probably using **70 to 90 percent** more power than new models, and you can make a significant cut in energy use by replacing them.

And because many retailers will take your old appliances and recycle them (as will some collectors, like 1-800-GotJunk), you don't have to fear that your old model will be lying in a landfill for thousands of years. Just ask a few questions before you buy.

· ·

Insulate your hot water heater with a water tank blanket. This will help your hot water tank to stay warm so your heater works less to heat your water. And by also lowering the water temperature to 120 degrees F, you can save up to $100 a year!

When you're shopping for appliances, think of two price tags. The first one covers the purchase price—think of it as a down payment.

The second price tag is the cost of operating the appliance during its lifetime. You'll be paying on that second price tag every month with your utility bill for the next 10 to 20 years, depending on the appliance.

When you do shop for a new appliance, heater or air conditioner, look for the Energy Star label. Energy Star products usually exceed minimum federal standards by a substantial amount.[1]

To help you figure out whether an appliance is energy efficient, the federal government requires most appliances to display the bright yellow and black EnergyGuide label.

Although these labels will not tell you which appliance is the most efficient, they will tell you the annual energy consumption and operating cost for each appliance so you can compare them yourself.

· ·

Clean the back and underside of your fridge at least once a year. All that dust makes it work much harder and waste more energy.

Saving energy is so important that Federal and State Governments have created tax credits[2] of up to $1,500 as well as other incentives[3] for purchasing Energy Star appliances. Energy Star even has a rebate locator.[4]

You might also qualify for rebates with your utility company, so be sure to check to see if they have any incentive programs for upgrading your appliances.

And with so many retailers offering great sales and incentives on appliances these days to get you to come to their store, now is a great time to save lots of money and energy!

Notes

1. Major appliances that carry the Energy Star label - http://www.energysavers.gov/tips/shopping_guide.cfm

2. http://www.energystar.gov/index.cfm?c=tax_credits.tx_index

3. http://www.energysavers.gov/financial/70020.html

4. Find a rebate - http://www.energystar.gov/index.cfm?fuseaction=rebate.rebate_locator

10.

Air Your Clean Laundry

According to Project Laundry List, commercial, industrial and residential clothes dryers use a whopping **15-20%** of domestic energy in the U.S.[1]

In 2007 alone, clothes dryers in U.S. homes emitted **54.72 million metric tons** of greenhouse gas-producing CO_2.

If all Americans used a clothesline or folding drying racks just once a week, *the savings would be enough to close several power plants!*

The Benefits of Using a Clothesline

According to Department of Energy statistics[2], about 5.8 percent of electricity use in your home goes towards the clothes dryer. It typically costs 30 to 40 cents to dry a load of laundry in a residential electric dryer and approximately 15 to 20 cents in a gas dryer.

Over its expected lifetime, the average clothes dryer will cost you approximately **$1,500** to operate. Using a clothesline will not only reduce the need for energy derived from fossil fuels, but also save you money.

Place your drying rack over your heating register during the winter to dry your clothes faster and humidify the room at the same time!

If you live in a community that has restrictions on clotheslines, consider getting a large, folding drying rack and putting it outside. You can also hang your clothes to dry indoors using an indoor clothesline, folding rack or a rack that mounts over your tub.

Hanging wet clothes to dry indoors can be a great way to provide added humidity in the winter for cold and arid climates (removing the need for an additional appliance, the humidifier); however, in the Pacific Northwest and other locations prone to indoor mold, you should be careful before erecting a clothesline or rack in the basement.

The Greenest Laundry

Sometimes when you dry your clothes outside they can get stiff. Adding **1/2 cup of vinegar** to the rinse cycle of your washing machine will save you from needing to buy a toxic chemical fabric softener.

Vinegar works naturally to soften your clothing and has the added benefit of breaking down laundry detergent very effectively. This means less detergent-sensitive allergies for families with sensitive skin.

Don't be put off by the fragrance of vinegar. The odor disappears when the vinegar dries.

To prevent wrinkles, "snap" your clothes. You want to shake them one time so hard that they make a cracking sound. Then hang the clothes carefully. You can even use a hanger on the clothesline to save yourself a step.

To make your laundry *completely* eco-friendly, wash full loads of clothes in cold water using a non-toxic, biodegradable laundry detergent with a vinegar rinse, then hang your clothes out to dry in the sun.

If everyone in the U.S. used a clothesline or a drying rack just once a week, we could make a huge difference in reducing the damage we are doing to our environment with our dependence on fossil fuels—which is not only important for the planet, but is absolutely vital for the health of our families and communities too.

Notes

1. Project Laundry List - http://www.laundrylist.org/

2. http://www.eia.doe.gov/emeu/recs/recs2001/enduse2001/enduse2001.html

11.

Leasing the Sun

Solar photovoltaic panels for your home can be expensive, requiring up-front investments of thousands of dollars. Even after federal and local tax rebates, it can take years for that investment to pay itself back to the homeowner in locally generated electricity.

Fortunately, more and more states are authorizing **solar leasing companies**, making solar energy as affordable as your monthly electric bill!

Installing solar panels to generate your home electricity has many benefits for you, our country, and our planet:

- **Protects you from escalating energy costs** - Electricity gets more expensive every year. Over the last 35 years, the average annual rate increase has been 6.5% (high energy users have seen substantially greater increases).

- **Supports clean energy** - The average solar PV residential system (based on 5kW), would save nearly 175 tons of carbon dioxide over its 30-year lifespan, equivalent to removing 32 cars from the road. It takes approximately 4,487 new trees to absorb that much carbon dioxide produced by fossil fuels.

- **Adds value to your home** - The value of a solar system is added to the appraised value of your property and does not increase your property taxes. Solar is one of the few home improvements that can be justified in terms of return on invested dollar.

- **Provides unlimited power** - Solar is a truly renewable and sustainable source of energy. It reduces your dependency on fossil fuels and produces your own electricity while reducing your carbon footprint. One of the side benefits is that with photovoltaic panels, homeowners have the ability to generate excess electricity during the day and sell it to the utility company through "net metering", i.e., you run the meter backwards.

- **Reduces the need for additional power plants** - Your utility company's peak demand is during the day. Meeting peak demand is how utility companies justify more power plants. On the hottest days, the oldest, dirtiest power plants are cranked up.

  Through net metering, you'll sell the output of the photovoltaic panels to the utility. This is even more efficient because most people are at work during peak hours, and don't need the energy their solar panels are generating at home.

  With enough people net metering, we will reduce the need for additional power plants that are only used to meet peak demand. That will protect the environment for everyone and help keep rates from going up too fast.

- **Rebates and tax credits are available** - Various financial incentives are available from the State and Federal governments to encourage investment in solar energy.

Solar Power Purchase Agreements

A power purchase agreement (PPA) is a type of solar financing where a private solar company owns, monitors and maintains the solar panels and equipment on your property, and you pay for the solar energy it produces, much like you pay your existing power company now.

Sometimes a PPA's rate is flat and sometimes it's calculated to rise slightly over the years, but unlike utility company rates, your PPA rate is **pre-negotiated for the lifetime of the agreement** (usually 15 to 20 years).

You can even pre-pay for all the energy you will need up front, locking in today's prices for decades to come!

This means you get clean, renewable solar energy at a set rate, instead of dirty, coal-fired grid power with rates that can go up at any time and by any amount.

With a PPA, you know exactly how much you'll be paying for your energy for as long as you have it.

If you can lock in an energy rate equal to or lower than your current monthly electricity bill, a PPA could save you thousands of dollars down the road!

Solar Panel Leasing

A solar panel lease is much like a car lease. Someone else owns, monitors and maintains the equipment, and you pay a monthly fee to lease it. Since your electricity is virtually free, the monthly payments for solar leases are often lower than your current electricity bill. There are even programs for renters where the panels are installed non-invasively on the property.

A solar lease differs from a solar power purchase agreement (PPA) in that you are leasing the *equipment*, whereas with a PPA, you're paying for the *energy* the panels produce.

However, similar to a PPA agreement, the advantage of a solar lease is that instead of making a large upfront investment in solar panels, you can get started for little to no money down.

Figuring out if a solar lease is worthwhile is easy: If the monthly lease payment is *less* than what you're currently paying for electricity, leasing probably makes financial sense for you. You'll be able to start saving money from the first day your panels are installed, for little to no up-front invest-ment.

When your lease is over (leases can vary in terms from 10 to 20 years), you'll have a few options. You can renew the lease for a new amount of time, buy out the system at fair market value, or ask your leasing company to remove the system. If you move before your lease is over, you can trans-fer the lease to the new owners.

Owning Versus Leasing?

If you plan to stay in your home a long time and can afford the up-front cost of solar panels, it may make more financial sense to buy them yourself because the total return on your investment is most likely going to be greater.

What you give up is the hassle-free aspect of leasing because the leasing company monitors, maintains, insures, and guarantees the production of the system.

Each state has its own rules regarding PPAs and solar leasing programs, and there are several states now with incentive programs available, so check with your local Department of Energy or utility to see what they offer.

There are also many different solar companies out there providing services with many different lease terms and fee schedules. Be sure to read the fine print on any lease and do your homework on any company you choose to do your installation.

· ·

If the monthly lease payment is less than what you're currently paying for electricity, leasing probably makes financial sense for you.

Shopping for Solar Leases and PPAs

When you're gathering quotes on solar leases, be sure to get good answers to the following:

- What will my monthly payments be?

- Will those payments go up over time and if so, by how much?

- What's the total cost of the lease over its entire lifetime?

- How does that compare to purchasing the same size system?

- What's my short term and long term ROI on the lease/PPA?

- If I want to buy the solar system at some point, what are my options?

- If I decide to buy the system at fair market value, how is that value determined?

- How does this leasing/PPA provider handle the solar rebates and incentives associated with installing the system?

- What happens with my panels if I move?

Here are a few national solar organizations to get you started with putting solar panels on your home. (Though don't forget to look up local companies in your state!):

- **PureEnergies.com** is a solar advocacy group that can help you determine if your roof is appropriate for solar panels. From there, they can connect you with solar installers in your region.

- **SolarSavingsAmerica.com** connects customers with solar panel installers and various incentive programs that make going solar more afford-able.

Can't Do Solar? You Can Still Get Your Power from Renewable Energy!

Can't put a solar panel on your home? You can still get your home (or business) electricity from re-newable sources like solar and wind.

Increasingly, electricity customers around the nation can choose where they would like their electricity to be supplied from, either as retail power markets open to competition or when utili-ties develop green pricing programs.

More than 50% of retail customers in the United States now have an option of purchasing a green power product *directly from their electricity sup-plier.*

By choosing to purchase your electricity from a green source like solar, wind, or geothermal, you can support increased development of renewable energy sources, which can reduce our need for fossil fuels such as coal, oil, and natural gas.

Greater reliance on renewable sources also provides jobs and other economic benefits to your state, and can improve our national energy security.

If retail electricity competition is allowed in your state, you may be able to purchase green power from an alternative electricity supplier. Some states have already implemented electricity competition.

Check the DOE Green Energy map to see the green power options your state offers.
(www.apps3.eere.energy.gov/greenpower/buying/)

Here are a few national and regional green power suppliers that offer renewable energy credits (RECs) through your existing utility company:

- **ArcadiaPower.com**

- **PEAR-Energy.com**

- **GreenMountain.com**

- **JustEnergy.com**

- **CommunityEnergyInc.com/**

- **EthicalElectric.com**

Even if your state is not implementing electricity market competition, you may still be able to purchase green power through your utility company.

More than 850 power companies in nearly every state offer "green pricing" programs that enable you to pay a little more to get your energy from renewable sources.

Call your power company to ask if they have a green power program you can join.

Many utility companies offer programs where you can get some or all of your electricity from renewable wind or solar. Be sure to ask!

Power in Your Own Hands

Installing solar panels on your home can make a real difference in reducing your bills and the ecological damage our dependence on fossil fuels creates—which is not only important for the planet, but is absolutely vital for the health of our families and communities too.

With solar leases, clean energy and greater self-sufficiency is within reach of more people than ever. Maybe even you!

12.

Water Conservation Saves More Than Water

Did you know that America faces a water-supply crisis? Less than 2% of the Earth's water supply is fresh water, and yet we're using and polluting our water faster than we can replenish our clean supply.

Today, the average American uses approximately **140-160 gallons** of water per day, so it's more vital than ever that we reduce our water usage as much as possible so we have enough for tomorrow.

The Nature of the Water Crisis

Robert Glennon, author of *Unquenchable,* tells us he believes Americans need a *moral compass* and the political will to prevent the water crisis from becoming a catastrophe.

Wasteful over-consumption of fresh water for agriculture, power generation, fracking, industry, and homes has led to grave reduction of ground-water, threats to rivers, and mortal danger to many of the nation's lakes.

Much of the blame for this state of affairs lies with uncontrolled growth in the nation's South and Southwest.

For example, desert cities such as Las Vegas have no water of their own, yet—conservation efforts notwithstanding—use lavish amounts of water serving tourists, including huge fountains.

And Phoenix households attempting to maintain lawns and golf courses in the middle of the desert draw down the finite resources of ever-shrinking Lake Mead. But the problem is not isolated just to hot, arid states.

Many states compete with one another over water allocation, and this conflict will only increase as our fresh water supplies diminish even further.

Desalination offers little immediate hope because of economic and ecological barriers. But there are some possible reforms we can enact *now* to decrease our fresh water consumption.

· ·

You can save a lot of water by placing a bucket under your faucet to catch the water as you wait for your shower to warm up. Use the saved water on your houseplants or garden.

Some, such as waterless toilets, are technological innovations. Others, such as restructuring sewer systems, require governmental intervention.

And, most importantly, we need to give people incentives to do many of the things we already know how to do to conserve water, like using drip irrigation instead of sprinklers or turning off the faucet while you brush your teeth.

Saving Water Starts at Home

Saving water is even more important if you live in a dry climate where there are water restrictions or drought conditions, like San Diego, Phoenix, or Denver.

But even if you live where rainfall is plentiful, a few easy changes can save you at least **$200 per year** on your water and sewer bills, and help protect our precious water supplies from depleting too quickly.

Try these water conservation tips that could save you hundreds of dollars a year—not to mention thousands of gallons of fresh water:

Dishwashers

If your dishwasher was built before 1994, buy a new energy- and water-efficient Energy Star-qualified model, and you'll save more than **$30 per year** in utility costs.

Many states and municipalities offer rebates or tax incentives for upgrading your dishwasher.[1]

Always wait until your dishwasher is full to run it. This way you can save even more water than hand-washing!

Faucets

If your bathroom and kitchen faucet pours out more than 2 gallons per minute, attach **low-flow faucet aerators.** They cost just a few bucks, and you'll save up to **$80 per year** on utility bills.

If you turn the sink off while you brush your teeth or scrub your hands, you'll save even more!

Showers

If your shower head blasts more than 3 gallons per minute, switch it out for a *low-flow* one. Most low-flow showerheads feel just as nice as the high-flow ones.

Since you'll also save energy (due to less hot water use), you'll shave about **$80 per year** off your utility bills. You can save even more if your shower takes less than 6 minutes!

Toilets

Compared to a pre-1993 3.5 gallon-per-flush toilet, a toilet marked with the EPA WaterSense label will use 1.3 gallons or less, saving up to **$90 per year**.

Many cities and water utilities offer local rebates if you change out your toilet to a low-flow or dual-flush model. Check with your utility.

· ·

Convert your existing toilet to a low-flow one by putting a plastic bottle full of sand or a brick placed in an airtight bag into the tank to displace the water.

You can also retrofit your tank with an inexpensive **dual-flush conversion kit** that will use less water when all you need to flush is urine.

Ever wonder why we use fresh, potable water to flush the toilet? What a waste! To really maximize your water savings, consider installing a Water-saver system that recycles the greywater from your bathroom sink by using it to flush your toilet.[2]

This greywater recycling system in combination with a low-flow, dual-flush toilet could save you hundreds of dollars and thousands of gallons a year!

Washing Machines

If your washing machine is more than 10 years old, a front-loading, high-efficiency Energy Star-qualified washer can save you about **$145 per year** between power and water bills.

Many states and municipalities offer rebates or tax incentives for upgrading your washing machine.[3]

Irrigation

Landscape irrigation is one of the biggest uses of household water during the summer, so anything you can do to save water outside your home will also save you at least **$75 a year**.

The first step to reducing landscape water use is to get rid of your lawn! A water-wise xeriscape using drought-tolerant, native plants is a lovely, green alternative to water-guzzling grass.

But for your vegetable garden, a series of rainbar-rels—or better yet, an above- or below-ground cistern—can capture rain water from your rooftop which you can then use to water your gardens for free, saving precious fresh water for cooking, drinking and bathing.

The average home rooftop can shed hundreds of gallons of water in a single rainstorm, so make sure your rainbarrel system or cistern can handle as much as you can afford to capture.

· ·

The average single rainstorm can release hundreds—if not thousands—of gallons of water onto your roof. Setting up a cistern or rain barrel system is one of the best ways to capture and preserve a lot of fresh water, fast.

You can also install a micro-irrigation system that targets just your plants and reduces the runoff and evaporation that wasteful sprinkler systems cause.

Many of these drip systems are very affordable, easy to install and highly efficient—they can even water your outdoor potted plants while you are away!

Conserving Water Helps Everyone

Since it takes energy to treat and heat our water, if just 1 out of every 100 American homes was retrofitted with water-efficient fixtures, *we'd save enough energy to power* **900 homes** *for a year.* So in every way it pays to conserve water.

After all, we can't live without it.

Notes

1. Find out if you qualify for rebates at www. energystar.gov/index.cfm?fuseaction=rebate.rebate_locator.

2. Learn more about Watersaver Aqus systems at www.treehugger.com/bathroom-design/watersaver-technologies-aqus-uses-sink-greywater-for-toilet.html.

3. Find out if you qualify for rebates at www. energystar.gov/index.cfm?fuseaction=rebate.rebate_locator.

13.

Reduce Your Transportation Footprint

Nothing would protect the environment and decrease our dependence on oil more than taking steps to reduce your transportation footprint. Transportation accounts for more than **30 percent** of U.S. carbon dioxide emissions.

In big cities like New York, Los Angeles, Chicago, Denver, and Washington, D.C., car pollution causes the grey smog that leads to hotter summers and those horrible orange, red and even *purple* air-quality days that cause asthma attacks in children and other health problems in adults.

That $3-4 (or so) a gallon you pay for gas does not even begin to cover the costs that the use of that fuel places on our economy. American's end up wasting 1.9 billion gallons of gasoline just sitting in traffic jams every year.[1]

This costs Americans like you and me over *$100 billion dollars per year* in fuel alone.

Then, If you factor in all of the hidden costs (externalities like climate change due to CO2 emissions, health care and lost work and school days due to smog-induced illness, pollution remediation costs, etc.), then the actual cost per gallon for gas is much closer to **$15 or $20 per gallon!**[2]

· ·

Fill up your tank either early morning or later at night, especially during hot weather. When gas is cooler, it is more dense. When it is hot, it expands so you get less as you pump.

No matter how you cut it, we are paying the real costs for every gallon of gasoline, one way or the other.

On the other hand, according to the American Public Transportation Association (APTA), public transportation in the United States saves approximately *1.4 billion gallons* of gasoline and about *1.5 million tons* of carbon dioxide annually.

Yet only 14 million Americans use public transportation daily, while 88 percent of all trips in the United States are made by car—and many of those cars carry only one person.

· ·

To save fuel, keep your tires inflated to the right PSI and rotated regularly. You can lose up to 6% in gas mileage for every pound of air pressure missing!

The Cost of Commuting on Our Health

Ground-level ozone, or "smog," is one of the most dangerous airborne pollutants.

Smog is made when nitrogen oxide (NOx), a by-product of burning fossil fuels like gasoline, combines with volatile organic compounds (VOCs) in the presence of sunlight, and becomes a colorless, odorless, gas.

Because of the role that sunlight plays in its production, ground-level ozone is more prevalent during the sunny months, from about mid-May until mid-September, which is often called the "smog season."

Every year, smog causes thousands of emergency room visits, costing our health care system *millions of dollars* to treat unnecessary respiratory illness.

What's worse is that about 9% of all non-accidental deaths are due to smog. The chemicals in smog also put you at significantly higher risk for rheumatoid arthritis, autoimmune disease, cancer, brain damage, heart disease, lung disease/COPD and asthma.[3]

Smog is Very Deadly to Children

Children are particularly vulnerable to smog because their lungs are still developing, they spend more physically active time outdoors, they breathe faster than adults and inhale more air per pound of body weight, and they are shorter than adults, which exposes them to more vehicle exhausts and heavier pollutants that concentrate at lower levels in the air.

In fact, in children, smog has been found to:

- aggravate asthma, leading to more frequent and severe asthma attacks;

- increase the number of respiratory infections;

- aggravate and induce allergies;

- increase school day absences; and

- increase emergency room visits, hospital admissions and premature deaths.

If you are going to be stopped for more than 30 seconds (except in traffic), turn off your engine. Idling your vehicle for longer than 30 seconds uses more fuel than it would take to restart the vehicle.

Idling your vehicle is a major source of smog, and is particularly an issue at schools because many bus drivers and parents sit with their vehicles idling while waiting to pick up their children, **creating a huge cloud of pollution for them to walk into as they leave the building.**

This is compounded by the fact that smog is already at its daily peak at the time when most parents are picking up their kids.

If you are going to be stopped for more than 30 seconds (except in traffic), **turn off your engine.** Idling your vehicle for longer than 30 seconds uses more fuel than it would take to restart the vehicle.

Solutions to Smog

Since ground level ozone and smog (not to mention tons of CO2) are created primarily by vehicles, the solution is simply to drive less, or travel in a vehicle that produces fewer or no emissions.

While living close enough to walk or bike to work is the healthiest, cheapest and most eco-friendly way to reduce your transportation footprint (not to mention improve your health), public transportation and carpooling/ride sharing are very good, frugal choices, too.

· ·

Reduce your driving speed by 5 m.p.h. and save up to $900 a year on gas!

Public transportation has the added benefit of creating jobs and improving commerce wherever it is supported.

In fact, every $1 billion of investment in the nation's public transportation infrastructure supports and creates **47,500 jobs** and yields **$3 billion** in increased business sales[4], largely due to increased foot traffic around trolley and subway stations and bus shelters.

In addition to public transportation, you can even further reduce your fuel costs and your contribution to smog pollution if you can arrange to work from home a few days a week.

Or, maybe you can team up with another family to do your shopping errands in one trip.

If the gas at your pump is rated E-15, leave. The E stands for ethanol and has 30% less energy than gasoline. Ethanol is a very wasteful form of fuel that uses up tons of good soil, water, oil and chemicals to make and displaces food crops needed to feed hungry people.

And if and when you are in the market for a new car, a hybrid or electric vehicle has very low or zero emissions and will save you a *ton* of money on fuel! They seem to be getting cheaper and more efficient with every new model.

Here's how commuting wisely could make a difference for your family:

- **Energy Independence.** If just one in 10 Americans used public transportation daily, U.S. reliance on foreign oil could decrease **40 percent.**

- **Safety.** Riding a bus is *79 times* safer than riding in an automobile, and riding a train or subway is even safer.

- **Health.** Studies have shown that people who use public transportation regularly tend to be healthier than people who don't, largely because of the exercise they get walking to and from bus stops, subway stations and their homes and offices.

- **Cost savings.** According to an APTA study,[5] families that use public transportation can reduce their household expenses by as much as **$6,200 annually**—more than the average U.S. household spends on food every year.

If you can bike or walk, you'll save *even more*.

· ·

Turning off your car's air conditioner and opening the windows can improve your fuel economy by more by than 20%! However, on the freeway, use the air conditioner if you have to, because the drag from the wind in your open windows will use up more gas.

But perhaps the best reason to leave the car at home is that on a bus, train or carpool, you can sit back, read the paper and avoid the stress and headache of dealing with rush-hour traffic.

And that's not only sustainable for our planet, but also for your peace of mind!

Notes

1. http://green.autoblog.com/2012/03/26/treasure-department-traffic-jams-waste-1-9-billion-gallons-of-g/

2. http://www.treehugger.com/energy-policy/true-cost-fossil-fuels.html

3. http://www.brighamandwomens.org/about_bwh/publicaffairs/news/pressreleases/PressRelease.aspx?PageID=473&issueDate=3/31/2009%20 12:00:00%20AM

4. http://www.apta.com/resources/reportsandpublications/Documents/twenty_first_century.pdf

5. http://www.apta.com/resources/reportsandpublications/Documents/twenty_first_century.pdf

14.

How Riding Your Bike Can Change the World

Transportation accounts for 20% of the American household budget, but this can be dramatically reduced by using a bicycle to get to work, or just to run errands.

A study of 11 Midwestern cities[1] found that if citizens switched to bikes for half of their short trips, they'd create a net societal health benefit of **$3.5 billion** per year from the increase in air quality and **$3.8 billion** in savings from health care costs associated with better fitness and fewer mortalities from a decreased rate of car accidents.

The researchers said their figures were conservative, but those are some pretty significant savings!

Because of these benefits, many cities are adding more and more bike lanes, and there are now bike paths stretching across most suburban areas as well.

Portland, OR, one of the most bike-friendly cities in the nation, expects to save over **$400 million** in health care costs alone as a result of their investment in biking infrastructure for their citizens!

Cycling Up

What's not to love about a bike? It's low-cost transportation powered by renewable energy, a low-impact exercise for almost everyone in the family to enjoy, and an *essential* ingredient to creating cleaner, healthier, more sustainable cities.

If you don't have a bike, you can easily get a very nice used one cheaply from Craigslist, Ebay, or the local paper. You can also rent one from a local bike shop or from bike sharing sites like Spinlister.com.

But if you have money to spend, or special needs, you can go so far as to get a super-cushy, *bamboo* comfort-cycle with solar-charged battery assistance to get you up the hills without breaking a sweat!

In fact, the new whisper-quiet *electric-assisted* bikes make bicycling accessible to more people than ever!

And these days, you can also find trailers of all types to schlepp everything from kids to groceries to golf clubs—making your bike a truly useful form of transportation.

Biking for just 30 minutes a day can save you an average of $500 in healthcare costs. And if you can bike to at least a few of your errands, you'll save a ton on gas and car upkeep costs too!

Bikes and Personal Sustainability

When the weather isn't too hot, it might be a good idea to take that bicycle for a spin as often as you can. Inactivity-related diseases (like heart disease, diabetes, hypertension, and even cancer) are the top killers in the United States.

But by adding just 30 minutes of exercise to your day—perhaps by bicycle—you can save an average of **$544 per person per year,** just in health costs!

If you move to or live somewhere where you can commute to work or run errands by bicycle, on top of the health savings, you will also save **tons** of money on gas, parking and automobile maintenance.

And if you are a two-car family, you could conceivably get rid of one car—and it's massive expense—if you arranged your life to make bicycle commuting possible.

What would you do with the several thousand dollars a year in savings that not needing an extra car would give you?

And as an added perk, bicyclists also save time during rush hour when they can actually out-pace cars in urban areas.

Traveling by bike not only gives you great physical and financial benefits, but also allows you to see the world in a different way.

Biking is slower, and you can wave hello to a neighbor or stop whenever you want to look around at new things and explore.

These days, slowing down and de-stressing may be the most important benefits of bicycling of them all.

Notes

1. http://www.ncbi.nlm.nih.gov/pmc/?term=10.1289/ ehp.1103440

15.

100 Things You Can (and Should) Compost

Composting is a sacred act. A person who composts is a thoughtful shepherd over the transformation from life into death into life again.

Without the holy cycle of decay and rebirth that the composter harnesses for her garden, life on this planet could not exist.

It is completely unsustainable for us to squander this essential resource and further deplete our precious topsoil by throwing our food and yard waste into landfills.

For your soil, there is no better ingredient than compost, whether you till it into your garden beds or use it as mulch around shrubs and trees, it is considered *essential* to organic and sustainable food production.

Once it's in the soil, finished compost—or **humus**—increases fertility, adds both micro- and macronutrients, buffers pH, prevents diseases, and improves soil structure.

Without compost, soil is just dead, inert mineral dust. Composting is not only essential for healthy plants and soil, but it can also **remove 20-50% from your household waste stream**, reducing the burden on landfills while replenishing your lawn, trees, houseplants, or garden for **free**.

And if you pay for trash pick-up, composting can save you a lot of money there, too.

Getting Started

A compost pile can be as easy as starting a heap of veggie scraps, dead leaves, and grass clippings in the far corner of your yard, but most people like to contain their compost in a compost bin.

There are many different kinds of compost bins to fit every living situation: simple pallet bins, tumblers that make turning the compost easy, towers for urban yards and small spaces, and even worm composters that will make fast, odorless work of all your table scraps in the space under your kitchen sink.

Select the bin style that works for you, and install it near the garden, away from your house.

Once you have reached a critical mass of scraps in your bin (usually about a cubic yard of material or a 3'x3'x3' pile), it will begin to noticeably break down.

After everything has decomposed and transformed into dark, rich-smelling, crumbly humus (see picture above), you can sprinkle it around your trees, lawn, garden or houseplants to help them grow.

Considered "black gold" by most gardeners, even if you don't garden yourself, you could easily give your compost away to your neighborhood green thumb! She'd be so grateful. Avid gardeners never seem to have enough compost.

· ·

Shred, tear or chop your compostable items into the smallest pieces you can manage. They will decompose much faster and more evenly.

100 Things You Can Compost

The basics of composting are simple. Almost anything natural or plant-based can be composted; just **don't add meat or a lot of fat**, because as they decompose, they will create a smell that will bring every critter for miles to your yard!

Always remember that an effective compost pile is a careful balance of **dry or brown** things that contain **carbon** (like leaves or paper) and **wet or green** things that contain **nitrogen** (like food scraps or rabbit droppings).

So, for example, if you add a lot of shredded paper or cardboard to the pile, you will need to balance it with a nice heap of fresh grass clippings or horse manure, and probably some water from the hose so things don't get too dry.

And, don't forget that the *smaller* you can shred or chop your compostable items before you put them into the pile, the *faster and more evenly* they will decompose.

It's really worth the extra effort to chop and shred if you plan to use your compost for vegetable gardening, or, simply compost tough, slow things like tree branches and old rope in a separate pile.

The following list is meant to get you thinking about your compost possibilities. Imagine how much trash we could prevent from going into the landfills if each of us just decided to compost a few more things!

From the Kitchen

1. Fruit and vegetable scraps

2. Egg shells (crushed)

3. Coffee grounds

4. Coffee filters

5. Tea bags (Make sure they are made of natural materials like hemp or cotton, and not rayon or other synthetics. If in doubt, just open it and compost the tea leaves alone.)

6. Loose leaf tea

7. Spoiled soy/rice/almond/coconut milk

8. Used paper napkins and paper towels

9. Unwaxed cardboard pizza boxes (ripped or cut into small pieces)

10. Paper bags (shredded)

11. The crumbs you sweep off of the counters and floors

12. Cooked pasta

13. Cooked rice

14. Stale bread, pitas, or tortillas

15. Stale tortilla chips or potato chips

16. Spoiled pasta sauce or tomato paste

17. Crumbs from the bottom of snack food packaging

18. Paper towel rolls (shredded)

19. Stale crackers

20. Stale cereal

21. Cardboard boxes from cereal, pasta, etc. (Remove any plastic windows and shred)

22. Used paper plates (as long as they don't have a waxy coating)

23. Nut shells (except for walnut shells, which are toxic to plants)

24. Tofu and tempeh

25. Seaweed, kelp or nori

26. Unpopped, burnt popcorn kernels

27. Old herbs and spices

28. Stale pretzels

29. Stale candy (crushed or chopped)

30. Stale protein or "energy" bars

31. Pizza crusts

32. Old oatmeal

33. Peanut shells

34. Cardboard egg cartons (cut them up)

35. Stale pumpkin, sunflower or sesame seeds (chopped up so they can't sprout)

36. Avocado pits (chopped up so they don't sprout)

37. Wine corks (chop up so they decompose faster)

38. Moldy cheese (in moderation)

39. Melted ice cream (in moderation)

40. Old jelly, jam, or preserves

41. Stale beer and wine

42. Toothpicks

43. Bamboo skewers (break them into pieces)

44. Paper cupcake or muffin cups

From the Bathroom

45. Used facial tissues

46. Hair from your hairbrush

47. Trimmings from an electric razor

48. Toilet paper rolls (shredded)

49. Old loofahs (cut up, natural only)

50. Nail clippings

51. Latex condoms

52. 100% cotton cotton balls

53. Cotton swabs made from 100% cotton and cardboard (not plastic) sticks

54. 100% cotton tampons and sanitary pads (including used)

55. Cardboard tampon applicators

56. Menstrual blood

57. Urine

From the Laundry Room

58. Dryer lint (from clothes made of cotton and other *natural* fabrics)

59. Old/stained cotton clothing and jeans (ripped or cut into small pieces)

60. Cotton fabric scraps (shredded)

61. Old wool clothing (ripped or cut into small pieces)

62. Very old cotton towels and sheets (shredded)

If most of your clothing is made from synthetic materials like rayon or spandex, you should skip composting your dryer lint. It simply won't decompose. Use the dryer lint from your towels or jeans loads instead.

From the Office

63. Bills and other plain paper documents (shredded)

64. Envelopes (shredded, minus the plastic window)

65. Pencil shavings

66. Sticky notes (shredded)

67. Old business cards (shredded, as long as they're not glossy)

Around the House

68. "Dust bunnies"

69. Contents of your vacuum cleaner bag or canister (Pick out any inorganic stuff, like pennies or Legos.)

70. Contents of your dustpan (again, pick out any inorganic stuff)

71. Newspapers (shredded or torn into smaller pieces)

72. Junk mail (shredded, remove coated paper and plastic windows)

73. Subscription cards from magazines (shredded)

74. Burlap sacks (cut or torn into small pieces)

75. Old rope and twine (chopped, natural, unwaxed only)

76. Leaves trimmed from houseplants

77. Dead houseplants and their soil

78. Flowers from floral arrangements

79. Natural potpourri

80. Used matches

81. Ashes from the fireplace, barbecue grill, or outdoor fire pits (in moderation)

82. Grass clippings

83. Dead autumn leaves

84. Sawdust (from plain wood that has NOT been pressure-treated, stained or painted)

Party and Holiday Supplies

85. Wrapping paper rolls (cut into smaller pieces)

86. Paper table cloths (shredded or torn into smaller pieces)

87. Crepe paper streamers (shredded)

88. Latex balloons

89. Jack O'lanterns (smashed)

90. Those hay bales you used as part of your outdoor fall decor (broken apart)

91. Natural holiday wreaths (chop up with pruners first)

92. Christmas trees (chop up with pruners first, or use a wood chipper, if you have one...)

93. Evergreen garlands (chop up with pruners first)

Pet-Related

94. Fur from the dog or cat brush

95. Droppings and bedding from your rabbit, gerbil, hamster, etc.

96. Newspaper/droppings from the bottom of the bird or snake cage

97. Feathers

98. Horse, cow or goat manure

99. Alfalfa hay or pellets (usually fed to rabbits, gerbils, etc.)

100. Dry dog or cat food, fish pellets

Just imagine if all of us kept so many things out of the landfills and returned their nutrients to the earth!

For a truly sustainable future that our *great-grand-children* can thrive in, this is what we will need to do, or we will deplete our precious soils into dust.

Good thing it is such an easy and frugal thing to do!

10 Things You Should Leave OUT of the Compost Pile

Even though technically you can compost anything that was once living, some things are better left out of the compost pile for the sake of better compost and less hassle. Here are 10 of them...

1. Dog and Cat Poop

Horse, cow, chicken and rabbit droppings are great additions to your compost pile. They will add nutrients and organic matter that will benefit your soil. However, it is not advisable to add the poop from dogs and cats (and other carnivores) to your compost. Their waste often contains micro-organisms and parasites that you do not want to introduce to the crops you will be eating.

If you do want to make use of your dog and cat poop, you must process them separately from your regular compost pile (there are special com-posters just for pet waste), and only use the resulting compost on flowers, shrubs and trees you won't be eating.

2. Tea and Coffee Bags

Coffee grounds and tea leaves definitely belong in a compost pile. They provide generous amounts of nitrogen, phosphorous and potassium, which are two elements essential to plants.

However, coffee grounds and tea leaves should only be added to compost if they are bag-less, or have been removed from their bags.

The bags that some coffee and tea products come in contain synthetic fibers that do not break down in a compost pile, and can contain chemicals you don't want in your soil.

Don't compost tea or coffee bags unless you are certain they are made from natural materials, like cotton or hemp.

3. Citrus Peels and Onions

While fruit and vegetables scraps from the kitchen are fundamental ingredients in a home compost pile, there are two iffy exceptions: *citrus peels and onions.*

"What?!" you say? Unfortunately, the natural chemicals and acidity in citrus peels and onions can kill worms and other microorganisms, which can slow down the decomposition in your pile.

Plus, unless you chop them into tiny bits, citrus peels can take forever to break down, which will delay how soon you can use your compost.

If you only occasionally throw citrus peels and onion scraps into your compost bin, it's no big deal, but if you vermicompost or have worm bins (which is an amazingly convenient and odor-free way to compost if you are in an apartment), then citrus peels, onions and garlic scraps are a no-no, because they will harm your worms.

(Personally, I usually put my onion scraps into the freezer to use when I make stock, and use citrus peels to make non-toxic DIY house cleaning sprays instead.)

4. Fish and Meat Scraps

While technically they will decompose just fine, you really don't want to add fish and meat scraps to the compost pile.

Fish and meat are organic and will add nutrients to your garden, but unfortunately their smell will act like a magnet for any rats, mice, foxes, raccoons, or cats in the neighborhood (or even coyotes and bears, depending on where you live), who will ransack the compost to eat them.

The stink of rotting meat and fish could also really annoy you and your neighbors, too!

5. Glossy or Coated Paper

Many paper products are potential compost fodder, especially soy-ink newspapers, old paper towels and tissues and even shredded cardboard. They are from trees, after all!

However, paper that has been treated with plastic-like coatings to make it bright, colorful and glossy, like magazines, won't decompose properly, contains toxins, and is not appropriate for your compost pile.

6. Sticky Labels on Fruits and Vegetables

Those obnoxious sticky labels and price tags on fruit and vegetables are made of "food-grade" plastic or vinyl, and do not biodegrade. (See Glossy Paper, above.) They are also easy to miss, which means they often end up trashing up compost piles.

Municipal composters can't handle them, either. In fact, at least one waste management company says PLU stickers are their biggest source of compost contamination.[1]

Try to remove these stickers from fruit and veggie scraps before you put them in the compost pile.

7. Coal Fire Ash

The ash from coal fires or charcoal-briquet fires should not be added to your compost pile, as it contains so much sulfur as to make the soil excessively acidic, which will harm your plants.

Also, many charcoal briquets are treated with chemicals you really don't want in your compost, your garden or your food.

Wood fire ash from the fireplace can be added in moderation, but please put the coal and charcoal-briquet ash in the trash bin.

8. Sawdust From Treated Wood

While sawdust from untreated, natural woods can be a great addition to compost, if the wood has been treated with any kind of pressure treatment, varnish, stain or paint, you should never add the sawdust to your compost pile.

These toxic compounds won't break down in the composting process and can get into the soil, negatively affecting microorganism activity and plant health.

The sawdust from pressure treated wood alone contains arsenic and cadmium—two toxins you definitely don't want in your garden or your food!

Sawdust from treated wood also takes a very long time to break down because it is protected from decay by the chemicals put on it, which will delay how soon you can use your compost on the garden.

9. Large Branches

Large branches take forever to break down and will greatly delay your ability to use your compost in the garden. It may be a little extra work to cut down or chip your branches for the compost pile, but the smaller the pieces you add to your compost, the faster they will break down.

Alternatively, you can start a branch pile at the back of your lot, where you simply pile branches and let them rot over the course of a couple of years.

Branch piles also make great habitat for small creatures and snakes too, so be aware of your local fauna before you start one.

10. Synthetic Fertilizer

Synthetic fertilizers (like the blue Miracle stuff) introduce inorganic elements into the garden ecosystem.

Like taking a generic multivitamin instead of eating real, whole food, the form in which these synthetic fertilizers provide nutrients to the soil is not natural. This can actually kill the microorganisms in your compost and your soil, which will ultimately affect the health of your plants.

Compounds in synthetic fertilizers, such as heavy metals, will also leach through the soil into the water table, as well as upset the natural balance of nutrients in the soil and increase salinity.

Stick to natural ingredients for your compost pile.

Notes

1.   http://tamwasteremoval.com/faqs/compost-faqs/

16.

Fall is For Tree Planting

Autumn is the optimal time to plant trees in most parts of the country.

As mundane as it may seem compared to solar panels and organic gardening, the reason why we should plant more trees is because it is one of the most powerful ways to make a personal difference for the environment.

And it's a fun and educational activity to do with kids, too.

Why We Should Plant More Trees

As we learned in third grade biology, trees are essential to life. They create the very air we breathe and filter air pollution.

What you may not know is that trees also build soil and help soak up storm water before it can create a flood. They also offer energy-saving shade that reduces global warming and creates habitat for thousands of different species.

Trees also help to reduce ozone levels and heat islands in urban areas, cooling city streets, and cleaning up city air.

Most importantly, trees sequester carbon, helping to remove carbon dioxide and other greenhouse gases from the air, which cools the earth. In fact, a mature (30+ years old) canopy tree absorbs enough carbon and releases enough oxygen to sustain two human beings!

The carbon storage capacity of forests is approximately *three times* as large as the pool of carbon in the atmosphere. If forests are changed, cut back, or eliminated, the captured carbon *goes into the atmosphere as carbon dioxide (CO_2).*

Despite their importance to life as we know it, every year we cut down over **50,000 square miles** of forest worldwide for paper, agriculture, building materials and fuel.

That's an area the size of the state of Alabama! *Every year!*

The carbon release from deforestation accounts for **25 to 30 percent** of the four to five billion tons of carbon accumulating every year in the atmosphere from human activities.

It also leaves the ground bare and prone to flooding and dangerous erosion.

Much of this wouldn't be necessary if we reduced, reused and recycled more, cultivated hemp for fiber, and used sustainable and recycled materials in all our buildings.

But until this changes, *we need to put the trees back any way we can, as fast as we can!*

Support Tree Planting

There are many local, national and international organizations that plant trees, and because planting trees costs relatively little, donating to these organizations can make a big difference.

You can also have trees planted specifically to offset your personal carbon emissions from airplane or car travel.

These organizations can help you out:

- **AmericanForests.org**

- **InternationalTreeFoundation.org**

- **RainforestRescue.org.au** - Restores rainforest species in Australia, Sri Lanka and Indonesia

- **ClearSkyClimateSolutions.com** - Provides carbon offsets through reforestation projects

- **Terrapass.com** - Provides carbon offsets for flying, driving, etc.

- **CarbonFund.org** - Provides a variety of carbon offset projects to choose from.

- **Carbonify.com** - Tree planting for offsetting carbon emissions

Also check with your local environmental or parks department for tree planting organizations and events in your community.

Plant a Tree at Home

While supporting tree planting organizations is a great way to be eco-friendly, you can also make a difference in your community by planting trees on your own property.

A properly-planted, mature shade tree on the south or west side of your house can **save you up to 25%** on your summer air conditioning bills and increase your property value by **up to 20%** with its beauty.

That same tree will also help soak up storm water in the neighborhood, and contribute habitat for local wildlife. And if you plant a fruit or nut tree, you get food as an added bonus!

You really can't go wrong by planting trees!

How to Properly Plant a Tree

September through November is the *ideal time* for planting trees, shrubs and perennials because it allows the roots to become established before the ground freezes and winter sets in.

Trees and shrubs planted in the fall are also better equipped to deal with heat, pests and drought the following season.

Another great reason to plant your trees and shrubs in the fall is so you can select them by the fall colors they produce.

Cooler, wetter weather is the perfect time for tree planting, and seasonal rains can often provide all the water the tree needs to establish.

However, if the weather is dry you should make sure your shade trees get about **15-20 gallons of water a week,** until they go dormant for winter. Fruit trees and ornamental trees and shrubs can receive a little less.

This is easiest to accomplish by using a TreeGator irrigation device, which saves water by delivering it right to the root zone of your tree.

Avoid planting broad leaved evergreens like rhododendrons, azaleas, boxwoods and hollies in the fall, because they are not likely to survive winter cold and wind so soon after planting.

However, virtually all other temperate shade trees, ornamental/fruit trees, and perennials are perfect for planting in the fall, before the soil gets too cold too dig.

··

The proper way to place mulch around a tree is in a "doughnut" shape that doesn't allow the rotting mulch to come into contact with the living, growing tree bark. NEVER pile mulch around the trunk of your tree!

The Arbor Day Foundation has a great video series on how to properly plant a tree.

(Learn how to plant a tree at www.arborday.org/trees/video/howtoplant.cfm.)

Here are a few key tips for proper tree planting that you may not know:

1. A healthy tree's root system is just as wide as its canopy, so be sure to **plant your tree in a location far enough from your house** to accommodate both the **mature** breadth of the tree branches and the **mature** spread of the tree roots.

Especially consider where your water and sewer pipes are in your yard in relation to your tree's future root spread.

It would be awfully expensive and tragic to have to cut down a 30-foot tall, mature shade tree because its roots were breaking up your plumbing.

2. **Make sure your tree is planted at the exact same depth as it was planted in the pot or burlap sack it came in.** Planting a tree too deep is a leading cause of tree death because it smothers the roots and introduces moisture and fungus to the trunk.

Planting a tree too shallow will expose too much of the top of the root system to the elements. If you have to move the tree to place more soil beneath it or take some away to get the tree to sit at the right depth during planting, it is worth the work. *A tree can last for generations if you plant it right.*

3. **Never pile mulch around the trunk of your tree!** I know people do this all the time everywhere you go, but it is a very harmful practice for the tree and shortens its lifespan greatly.

While you should always mulch your trees, piling up the mulch around the trunk *like a volcano* introduces wood-rotting bacteria and fungus from the mulch directly to the living, growing bark of the tree. The moisture build-up and fungus will often girdle or kill the tree before it can reach maturity.

The proper way to place mulch around a tree is in a "doughnut" shape that doesn't allow the rotting mulch to come into contact with the living bark. (See image above.)

4. **Don't use stakes unless absolutely necessary.** If the tree is grown and dug properly at the nursery, staking for support will be unnecessary.

Trees establish more quickly and develop stronger trunk and root systems if they are *not* staked at the time of planting, but instead are allowed to adapt to local conditions.

However, protective staking may be necessary where lawn mower damage, vandalism, or windy conditions are concerns.

Make sure your new trees get about 20 gallons of water a week—more during the summer months. Make this easy by installing a TreeGator watering device.

This fall, consider planting a tree or two on your property, or help with a tree planting in your community.

And this holiday season, consider a generous donation to a non-profit that plants trees or does reforestation work. We all benefit greatly from living among more trees.

Saving Money on What You Buy

17.

Save with Spend-Fasting and The Compact

If you have ever abstained from eating anything for a while to prepare for a health procedure or religious occasion like Lent, Yom Kippur or Ramadan, you should be familiar with the concept of *fasting*.

Similar to a food fast, a **spend-fast** is simply abstaining from spending any *money* for a specific period of time.

For example, a 30-day spend-fast would mean that, for just a month, you would only spend money on the things you *truly need to live*—like toilet paper, groceries and doctor appointments.

You would refrain from buying any impulse and entertainment purchases—like potato chips, coffee drinks, movies, magazines, those cute earrings you saw in the store window, or take-out meals.

Spend-Fasting Helps Foster Mindfulness About Money

Doing this practice for just a week can really help you notice if you are spending your money *as a form of recreation.*

Spending money in and of itself has become an American hobby. We spend money on myriad conveniences and small comforts without even thinking about it; *we go shopping for fun and relaxation!*

And it seems if you want to do just about anything fun out of the house these days, you are expected to spend at least a little money.

How did this come to be? Could this be how we, as a nation, got in over our heads economically and environmentally, and came to live way beyond our collective means?

The generations that came before us would be appalled at the wasteful and profligate manner in which we use our money today. Our grandparents and great-grandparents lived very frugally, did their best to repair things before replacing them, and lived on only what they needed with few luxuries.

They certainly didn't try to fill their free time or their spirits with a trip to the mall or the purchase of the latest gizmo.

In fact, before rampant consumerism took over our culture, it was normal for people to regularly have potlucks and BBQs, take walks, visit neighbors, play music and sing, go to the library, make homemade cookies, watercolor, garden, and do lots of other wholesome, fun things that cost nothing and make family and community life feel meaningful and satisfying.

So if you want that sense of meaning for your family today, you must be willing to unplug from

our culture's current dependence on rampant consumerism.

· ·

The Story of Stuff" is a brilliant, upbeat little movie to share with your family about how reducing consumption can make us all healthier and wealthier. To watch, go to http://storyofstuff.org/movies/ story-of-stuff/.

The Rules of Spend-Fasting

There is one basic rule of spend-fasting, no matter how long you decide to do it:

Only spend money on things you genuinely need for your health, safety and well-being.

This means the list of things you *can* spend money on is much shorter than the list of things you *can't*.

During a spend-fast, the following are OK to spend money on:

- Mortgages, rental fees, leases, loans, utilities and other contractual payments

- School and school supplies (only required supplies, no luxuries)

- Medical, dental and optical insurance, appointments and prescriptions

- Gas, insurance and car repairs; public transportation fees

- Groceries to make three basic meals a day (no beverages, treats or snacks, unless whole fruit or made from scratch)

- Toilet paper and basic toiletries (no paper towels, perfumes, etc.)

- Underwear and socks, if needed

Just about everything else is off-limits for the duration of your fast. (Though use your discretion about things not on this list.

Only you can determine what you absolutely *must* spend money on each month.)

This means no movies, no take out, no new clothes... No visit to the salon or barber, no piles of packaged snack foods and treats in the cupboard, no "Mochaccinos" or fast food breakfast...

No shopping for *anything* but except exactly what you need to get by for the duration of your experiment.

....

Read your favorite newspapers or magazines online instead of buying the paper version. You can often get the latest issue from the library too. This saves not only money, but also trees, water and oil!

The Return on Your Investment

During a 30-day spend fast, you could potentially **save $200–500 dollars,** simply by not buying any of the miscellaneous impulse and entertainment buys you don't really need to be happy (but thought somehow you did).

Not only is a spend-fast a great *experiment* in reclaiming meaningful time with your family, but also really good for the environment and your wallet.

This means that not only do you save money by not buying stuff you don't really need, but *all the natural resources and fossil fuels that would have gone into getting, owning and eventually disposing of those items has been saved, too.*

Things can get a little tricky at times during a spend-fast. You will need to confront and unlearn old spending habits, and find new things to do with your time besides spending money.

Remember: Like any fast, it teaches a lesson, and it's only temporary.

I encourage you to try it for a full 30 days to work all the way through that initial learning curve you might experience. It's really worth it!

• •

If you need a shovel, circular saw or rototiller, see if a neighbor or someone on Neighborgoods.net, Nextdoor.com or Buy Nothing Project.org can help you before you buy a new one.

The Compact

After the Spend-Fast experiment (or perhaps instead), you might want to join something called **The Compact.**

The Compact started with a group of friends in San Francisco who pledged not to buy anything **new** (almost) for an entire year.

The only new products allowed by The Compact are food and bare necessities for health and safety —things like toilet paper, brake fluid & underwear.

In the effort to go without buying anything new; everything else you might need should come from places like FreeCycle, Craigslist, Neighborgoods. net, Nextdoor.com, BuyNothingProject.org, thrift stores and even dumpsters.

· ·

Buy it used. Anything—furniture, clothing, electronics—can be bought used in good shape. This saves money and saves one more thing from going to a landfill!

The Compact Yahoo Group (groups.yahoo.com/ group/thecompact/) has attracted over 10,000 members, and has spawned SubCompact cells operating across the country and the world. To join, all you have to do is make the pledge not to buy anything new for 365 days.

Whether you try a spend-fast or take the Compact, the true reward in spending less money is in spending more quality time with your friends and family, finishing things on the to-do list, cooking and eating together more, and generally enjoying life with less worry about your wallet.

And no amount of money can pay for that!

18.

A Credit Union is Much Greener Than a Bank

These days, it's almost impossible not to feel angry about the role that Wall Street, corporations and the Big Banks have had in crashing the economy, depressing wages and tanking the housing market.

We seem to be living in a Robber Baron-era paradigm wherein the harder Americans work, the more into debt we collectively descend.

While Bank of America, BB&T, Citigroup, Chase and their friends gave themselves grotesque raises and bonuses paid for with taxpayer bail-out money, Americans have endured subprime mortgage fraud, merciless or even fraudulent fore-closures,[1] and losing their retirement money, their jobs and their dignity.

And while most of us lose more of our health, wealth and security every day, Big Banks and Wall Street corporations are enjoying record profits that were basically stolen from the rest of us.

But if that isn't enough to make you mad, you should also know that environmental and human rights violations are widespread within the bank-ing industry due to the unsustainable (and often downright immoral) way in which they invest **your** money in order to make a profit for **their** share-holders.

According to Green America,[2] the worst social and environmental offenders are Citibank, Bank of America, Fidelity, JP Morgan, Vanguard, Suntrust and Wells-Fargo. But many other larger and mid-sized banks are pretty dirty, too.

For example, speculation in China's oil industry—whose proceeds directly fund the Sudanese army and Janjaweed militia which carries out the geno-cide in Darfur—is perhaps the most heinous of the banking industry's recent investments.

Here in the U.S., Citibank and JP Morgan have been accused of helping Enron doctor its books. And HSCB bank helped known drug cartels launder their money. And they each got off virtually Scot free!

These banks have also been criticized for profit-ing from apartheid in South Africa and supporting other abusive regimes around the world.

> It seems that wherever in the world people and planet are exploited for the sake of the easiest profit, you'll find a Big Bank in partner-ship with a corrupt regime.

Additionally, the banking industry finances de-velopment projects that are devastating to the environment but lucrative to shareholders, such as the construction of *coal-powered* energy plants, *mining and deforestation* in the Amazon River basin, *mountaintop removal* projects, *oil and gas drilling* in pristine wilderness and tribal lands, and more.

In fact, almost every major, for-profit, environmentally-destructive project on the planet was funded by Big Banks.

> *This means that Americans who bank at large institutions like Suntrust, Citibank or Bank of America, etc. are, in effect, funding these human and environmental atrocities.*

To get away with all of this, the Big Banks also use **your** money to lobby for policies, laws and candidates that deregulate their industry and protect their profit-at-all-costs agenda.

How do you think we got into this mess in the first place?

But you don't have to stuff your mattress with cash to escape the Big Banks and their shenanigans. Instead, you can do a lot of good with your money by investing it right in your community, right now.

Credit Unions

Credit unions are financial institutions formed by an organized group of people with a common bond. There are credit unions for teachers, members of the military, people who live in a certain area—almost every affiliation you could imagine.

Members of credit unions pool their assets to provide loans and other financial services to each other on a not-for-profit basis. This allows credit unions to pay dividends to their members (not shareholders) and offer them **lower loan rates, higher savings rates and fewer service fees.**

Credit unions have the smallest environmental footprint of all types of banks because they exist only for their members and are supported only by their members.

As opposed to large, national banks, you can be sure that the money you put in a credit union is not going to be invested in corporations that pollute the air and water, remove mountaintops for mining, make genetically-engineered seeds, tear down the rainforest, maintain concentrated livestock feeding operations, contaminate your water with fracking, or anything else destructive that you might not want to financially support.

Credit unions usually offer the lowest service fees and loan rates in the entire banking industry. They also typically offer the highest interest rates for your savings and CDs too. And that can save a lot of money!

Here is why a credit union is better than a bank, and will save you a lot of money, too:

Credit Unions - Member Owned

Banks - Private Corporations

Not-for-profit, credit unions exist solely for service and focus solely on serving their members.

In the business to make a profit and serves both stock holders and customers.

Any income is returned to members in the form of low or no service fees, low rates on loans and higher deposit rates.

Only stock investors get a share of the profits.

Credit Unions - Member Owned

Members elect a volunteer Board of Directors to represent their interests. Each member is an equal owner.

Deposits are federally insured by the National Credit Union Administration (NCUA) to at least $250,000 and insured up to $250,000 for Individual Retirement Accounts (IRAs).

Banks - Private Corporations

Have a paid Board of Directors who represents the investors. Only investors have voting rights. Customers have no voting rights, and no authority in the governance of the bank.

Deposits are federally insured up to $250,000 by the Federal Deposit Insurance Corporation (FDIC). However banks are free to use your money to gamble on risky investments.

Credit Unions - Member Owned

Like other not-for-profit institutions, credit unions are exempt from paying federal income tax. Credit unions do pay property and state taxes.

Financial cooperatives. Members pool their savings to provide low-cost loans and low-fee services to each other.

Banks - Private Corporations

Like other for-profit businesses, banks must pay taxes to the government, though there are considerable loopholes, rebates and even "bailouts" available.

Commercial businesses. Banks offer services to make a profit.

State and Public Banks

Once you have moved your bank accounts to a credit union (or even a small local, community bank in your town), consider advocating for the creation of a State or Public Bank in the state where you live.

The one state with the foresight to have their own bank and create their own credit (rather than beg Wall Street) is North Dakota[3]—the only state with a growing budget surplus and low unemployment during the Great Recession.

North Dakota is such a model for success[4] that other states are working on opening their own state-owned banks, including Oregon, Washington State, Massachusetts, Arizona, Maryland, New Mexico, Maine, California, Illinois, Virginia, Hawaii and Louisiana.

In California alone, a State Bank would save about $5 billion in interest costs every year with at-cost credit. This would potentially re-hire 20,000 laid-off teachers at $70,000/year and still have $1.5 billion left-over.

At-cost credit could also mean at-cost public mortgages (think 1-2% interest rate).

Online banking saves you time, money for stamps and travel, and reduces the amount of paper mail coming to your house. Many banks and credit unions also waive certain fees if you use their online banking services.

Making a Difference by Opting Out

Opting out of the Big Banking system by using a credit union is a lot like opting out of the Big Food system by growing your own and buying from local farmers. Both are necessary ingredients in creating a sustainable, more just society.

If you'd like to help end the irresponsible lending and gambling on human misery perpetuated by the Big Banks, and be sure that your money is only invested in sustainable, local projects, then vote with your dollars by banking at a credit union or small community bank.

Then, go vote at the polls for the creation of a state-owned or public bank where you live.

You can find other ways to green your finances by visiting **Green America** at www.greenameri-catoday.org/programs/responsibleshopper/live/banking.cfm.

Notes

1. http://www.care2.com/causes/bank-of-america-told-employees-to-make-foreclosures-happen.html

2. Find a socially and environmentally responsible bank - http://www.greenamericatoday.org/programs/responsibleshopper/industry/banking.cfm

3. http://www.motherjones.com/mojo/2009/03/how-nation%E2%80%99s-only-state-owned-bank-became-envy-wall-street

4. http://www.commondreams.org/view/2011/06/12-3

19.

30 Ways to Use Less Paper

Why should we care about our paper usage? Paper is pretty cheap and renewable, right? Unfortunately, paper is *substantially* more resource intensive than you would think.

Paper's Heavy Footprint

From cradle to grave, paper-making uses a tremendous amount of energy and natural resources. First, trees are cut down and the wood is chipped into small pieces. Then water and heat, and sometimes chemicals, are added to separate the wood into individual fibers.

The fiber is mixed with lots of water (and often recycled fiber), and then this pulp slurry is sprayed onto a huge flat wire screen which is moving very quickly through the paper machine. Water drains out, and the fibers bond together.

The web of paper is pressed between enormous machine rollers which squeeze out more water and press it to make a smooth surface. Heated rollers then dry the paper, and the paper is slit into smaller rolls, then into sheets, and removed from the paper machine.

Americans are the heaviest paper users in the world. The average American uses about seven trees[1] or an average of 700 pounds[2] in paper, wood, and other products made from trees every year. This amounts to about 2,000,000,000 trees and more than 90 million short tons of paper and paperboard annually!

This would be the same consumption for 6 people in Asia or 30 people in Africa. That's a lot of demand, and that demand has a powerful impact.

40% of the world's industrial logging goes into making paper, and this is expected to reach 50% in the near future.[3]

Paper production is the third most energy-intensive of all manufacturing industries, using over 12% of all energy in the industrial sector. The paper and pulp industry is also the fourth largest emitter of greenhouse gases in the manufacturing sector.[4]

Yikes!

Paper plantations are better than outright deforestation, but because plantation trees are planted in perfect rows, sprayed with herbicides and pesticides, and then harvested before maturity, these trees offer no habitat to wildlife and no benefits to the environment.

If that weren't bad enough, the use of toxic chemicals for pulping and bleaching paper, and the dangerous chemical pesticides and herbicides on fiber plantations lead to pollution that causes negative impacts on the health of paper company workers and communities downstream from mills.

In fact, the paper industry is responsible for the release of persistent toxic pollutants like chlorine, mercury, lead and phosphorus into the environment, resulting in a legacy of health problems including cancers, nerve disorders and fertility problems.

Chlorine bleaching is particularly widespread in the paper industry, which results in dangerous pollution. Chlorine is the building block of organochlorines, which include some of the most toxic compounds on earth, such as dioxins and furans.

In the U.S., in order to meet Environmental Protection Agency rules, most paper is now "elemental chlorine free" (ECF), which has led to a 94% reduction in dioxins, however the Environmental Protection Agency's own rules state that *there is no safe level of dioxin*. And the dioxins already created in earlier years can persist in the environment and in our bodies.

Dioxin is known to cause reproductive problems, including low sperm counts and endometriosis and is implicated in a range of other health problems including diabetes, hyperactivity, allergies, immune and endocrine system problems.

Not only is paper-making a very toxic business, in some regions of the world, the land rights of indigenous peoples and rural communities are violated in the course of activities by pulp and paper corporations.[5]

When paper companies are granted concessions to log forests and/or establish fiber plantations without gaining the full and informed prior consent of local communities or indigenous peoples with customary rights on that land, this is an abuse of the land rights of those people and communities. Unfortunately these abuses are far too widespread.

All in all, paper has a very heavy footprint.

Waste Not, Want Not

Though paper recycling rates in the U.S. have increased in recent years, paper still represents one of the biggest components of solid waste in landfills—26 million tons (or 16% of landfill solid waste) in 2009.[6]

Approximately 1 billion trees worth of paper are thrown away every year in the U.S., and commercial and residential paper waste accounts for *more than 40 percent* of waste going to the landfill.

When paper decomposes in a landfill, it releases methane, a greenhouse gas 23 times more potent than carbon dioxide. Eliminating this paper from our waste would greatly reduce methane emissions and nearly double the lives of current landfills.

Like food, paper has no business in a landfill.

For every ton of paper we recycle, we save:[7]

- 17 mature trees

- 7,000 gallons of water

- 380 gallons of oil

- 4,100 kilowatt hours of electricity—enough energy to power the average American home for six months!

- 3.3 cubic yards of landfill space

It really pays to recycle paper and use recycled paper products! But let's remember that recycling comes last in the triad of Reduce, Reuse, Recycle.

Recycling is a last resort.

Recycling is what we do with something when we have exhausted all opportunities to redesign, reuse or repair it, or to simply do without it altogether.

As a last resort, recycling paper is better than putting it in landfill for sure. *But we shouldn't believe that recycling will make that much of a difference.*

Recycling is Not Enough

To make a difference for the planet and the climate—and to save a lot of money too—reducing your "paper footprint" is the only way to go.

By using less paper, you can reduce your impact on forests, cut energy use and climate change emissions, limit water, air and other pollution and produce less waste. Reducing your demand for paper will also help lessen the social impacts and human rights abuses linked to paper production.

The climate benefits of reducing paper consumption are significant. If the U.S. cut its office paper use by just a mere 10 percent, or 490,000 metric tons, greenhouse gas emissions would fall by 1.45 million metric tons. *This is the equivalent of taking 280,000 cars off the road for a year.*[8]

Using less paper also helps ensure we use only our fair share of the earth's resources. Think how much better the world would be if the current amount of paper we produce were used to make books for schools in poor nations instead of wasted on unnecessary office printouts and junk mail.

Here are thirty ways you can cut your paper consumption for good.

Save Paper in Your Home

1. **Use cloth napkins.** They come in lots of colors and prints, and add an elegant touch to even the most modest of meals—and aren't you worth it? Try using a different color for every member of the family, and unless someone makes a big mess, wash them only once a week.

2. **Use rags or kitchen towels instead of paper towels.**

3. **Avoid using paper plates and cups.** Use durable, washable ones if you need something for a social occasion. (You can get a large set of cheap mix-matched dishes from the thrift store for BBQs and parties, and you can also ask people to bring their own plate and cup too!) If you must use paper plates, try to buy the type made with recycled content.

4. **Buy bulk foods using your own reusable containers** rather than buying packaged foods at the grocery store. Join or start a buying club and save even more paper (and money)!

5. **Use your own reusable bag** at *all* the stores you go to (not just the grocery store) and skip the paper bags.[9]

6. **Use reusable coffee filters** (metal mesh or unbleached cloth) instead of paper ones. White-paper coffee filters bleached with chlorine are not only bad for the environment, but some of the chlorine and dioxins can end up in your coffee.

7. **Use a handkerchief instead of tissues.**

8. **Use recycled toilet paper.** If every household in the United States replaced just one roll of virgin toilet paper with one roll of recycled post-consumer waste recycled toilet paper, 424,000 trees would still be standing.[10] Now think of how many rolls of toilet paper you use every year...

9. If you're feeling really gung-ho, **switch to "family cloth" or washable cloth wipes** in lieu

of toilet paper and baby wipes. Using family cloth is not only a major money saver and tree preserver, but cloth wipes are *way more comfortable too!* (*See how to do it in a way that isn't gross in the Notes.*[11])

10. And while your replacing paper in the bathroom, **consider using cloth menstrual pads or a silicone menstrual cup** in lieu of pads and tampons in paper packaging. These will save you hundreds of dollars a year, are usually a lot more comfortable, and have no bleaching toxins in them or risk of Toxic Shock Syndrome!

11. **Use cloth diapers instead of disposable ones.** The paper and wood pulp that go into disposables and their packaging make them not only a huge waste of trees, water, oil and energy, but they are also a vector for toxins against your baby's skin and an incredible waste of money.

    Don't worry about washing cloth diapers; it takes *far less water and energy*[12] to wash cloth diapers than it does to produce, transport, and then dispose of billions of disposables every year.

12. **Use a white board or the Notes application on your phone** for household lists, notes or announcements.

13. **Change your bills to "paperless" and pay them online or by phone.** Most companies will make this easy for you to do since an e-mail is a lot cheaper than postage. You can also set up automatic billing, which should be even lower stress (assuming that you can pay them) since it just automatically debits your bank account at billing time. Ask for paperless reports from credit cards and banks as well. Most banks offer this service through their websites or phone support.

14. **Save online receipts in a folder on your computer.** Print each receipt to a file (PDF, RTF, etc.), then place all the files in a folder. There are many print-to-file techniques available, though they depend on your computer's operating system and setup.

15. **Try to stop as much of your junk mail as possible.** Junk mail is responsible for the waste of at least 100 million trees a year, not to mention all the water, oil and energy that goes into

producing something that just ends up in the trash.

16. **Re-use one-sided paper for notes, sketches, etc.** You can even reuse paper from the re-cycling bin for this. Always use both sides of pieces of paper when you can.

17. **Be frugal about magazine subscriptions, newspapers etc.** Many newspapers and maga-zines have online versions, and often the online subscription is cheaper than the print version.

18. Unless you need a particular book as a ref-erence on your bookshelf (like a recipe or how-to book), **consider buying only digital books** and reading them on an e-reader.

    Digital book-reading devices and e-books have come way down in price, making it possible to save trees and have a vast library without having to pack dozens of boxes of books every time you move!

Save Paper at School or Work

19. **Bring a thermos or ceramic mug to the office** and use it for coffee instead of disposable

cups. Also bring a glass or water bottle to use at the water cooler.

20. **Skip the paper bags, plates and napkins at lunchtime**, and bring a reusable lunch bag, dish and cloth napkin to work.

21. **When buying paper, buy recycled when you can.** Try to get the highest "post-consumer content" percentage available.

22. **Think before you print.** Do you really need to print it? Many people have the habit of just clicking the print button whenever they want to read something. This is incredibly wasteful. Reading on a screen isn't perfect either, but it doesn't waste paper needlessly.

23. **If you only need one page of a document, only print that.** This is often very easy to do in the "Print" menu of whatever word processor (or Internet browser) you are using.

24. **When printing a web page, copy and paste the text into a word processor** so that it is formatted correctly for printing. Some websites even have a print button that will format the page for you. Printing web pages "as is" often

prints a lot of junk that you don't want, and can also use up expensive colored inks.

25. **Print on both sides of the paper** using the "duplex mode" on your printer. Most modern printers will do this.

26. **Adjust margins on your documents** so they take fewer pages to print. A smaller margin of .75 inch is becoming more common.

27. **Use Google Docs, Trello, Dropbox or other software** that allows you to collaborate on projects digitally instead of using paper. It is even possible to do editing and collaboration using standard word processors. For instance, you can use "Track Changes" in Microsoft Word to put editing marks in documents, and view the editing changes that have been made by other people.

28. **Use e-mail rather than paper mail** whenever you can. Store your files electronically, instead of on paper, and invest in good backups. Most businesses and even governments are in the process of transferring over to electronic services. This will drastically reduce the costs of postal service as well.

29. **Use a USB data stick, also known as a "thumb drive,"** to move around or share electronic documents rather than printing them. Encourage people to bring their reports to meetings in electronic format, and for attendees to bring electronic storage of their own (or share via an Internet-based document storage). Many companies are utilizing an "intranet" now, allowing them to securely distribute documents to company employees only.

30. **Don't put your mailing address on your business cards;** only put e-mail, website (if applicable), and phone. This forces people to contact you through these electronic media.

Saving paper in your home, school and office not only conserves forests, energy, soil, water and air, it can save you a ton of money too.

Notes

1. http://www.recycling-revolution.com/recycling-facts.html

2. http://www.tappi.org/paperu/all_about_paper/faq.htm

3. http://www.worldwatch.org/node/850

4. http://environmentalpaper.org/our-resources/epn-reports/2007-state-of-the-paper-industry/

5. http://environmentalpaper.org/wp-content/uploads/2012/02/social-impacts-fact-sheet.pdf

6. http://environmentalpaper.org/our-resources/epn-reports/2011-state-of-the-paper-industry/top-ten-indicators/

7. http://www.epa.gov/osw/conserve/materials/paper/basics/index.htm

8. http://environmentalpaper.org/wp-content/uploads/2012/02/paper-efficiency-fact-sheet.pdf

9. Here's one way to remember your reusable bags - http://www.smallfootprintfamily.com/how-to-remember-your-reusable-bags

10. http://www.acoolerclimate.com/articles/prevent-global-warming-paper-recycling-facts/#ref2

11. Family cloth made easy - http://www.frugallivingnw.com/reusable-cloth-toilet-paper-faqs/

12. Dangers of disposable diapers - http://www.smallfootprintfamily.com/dangers-of-disposable-diapers

20.

20 Ways to Use Less Plastic

Plastic seems to be an unavoidable part of modern life in the U.S. Therefore, it is extra important to separate the "good" plastics from the ones that can leach harmful chemicals like BPA, BPS, phthalates, xenoestrogens, lead and antimony into food, beverages and the environment.[1]

These toxic chemicals—found in the majority of plastic, PVC and vinyl items produced today—have been linked to obesity, enlarged male breasts, earlier puberty in girls, and increased incidence of breast, prostate and other cancers.

In fact, they are so toxic, these plastic additives have been banned in Europe, Canada, China, and an increasing number of cities and states in the U.S.

Most of us know by now to avoid toxic, BPA-ridden plastic beverage bottles, plastic food storageware, plastic wrap and resealable (or zip-per-lock) food storage bags. (If you didn't know that, now you do!)

But, plastic is everywhere, so toxins can be found in the places you might not know about, like:

- BPA-free plastic bottles (BPS),

- the inside lining of nearly all canned food, soda and baby formulas (BPA/BPS),

- canning jar lids (BPA),

- toothbrushes and toothpaste tubes (BPA),

- plastic lunchboxes and toys (phthalates and lead),

- dental sealants and composite fillings (BPA/BPS),

- plastic and vinyl jewelry, purses, shoes and other fashion items (phthalates, mercury and lead),

- cash register receipts (BPA/BPS), and more.

One way to sort out which plastics are safer than others is by checking the Plastic ID Code on the bottom of the item, which is that little number inside the triangle that tells you if you can recycle it.

What Do The Numbers on Plastic Containers Mean?

#1 – PET or PETE (polyethylene terephthalate)

PET is used for water and soft drink bottles, mouthwash bottles, containers for condiments like nut butters and ketchup, and TV dinner trays. PET is considered safe, but it can actually leach the toxic metal antimony, which is used during its manufacture.

One study[2] that looked at 63 brands of bottled water produced in Europe and Canada found concentrations of antimony that were more than 100 *times* the typical level found in clean groundwater (2 parts per trillion).

The study also found that the longer a PET bottle sits on the shelf—in a grocery store or your pantry—the greater the amount of antimony present. It is also thought that the amount of antimony leaching from these PET bottles increases the more they are exposed to sunlight, higher temperatures, and varying pH levels.

Brominated compounds have also been found to leach into PET bottles.[3] Bromine displaces iodine in the body, and is a central nervous system depressant. It can accumulate over time, and trigger paranoia and other psychotic symptoms. **Avoid if you can.**

#2 – HDPE (high-density polyethylene)

HDPE is used in butter tubs, milk jugs, juice, household cleaner and shampoo bottles, as well as cereal box liners and grocery bags. It is often considered a low-toxin plastic, but like almost all plastics, it has been found to release estrogenic chemicals.

In one study, 95 percent of all plastic products tested were positive for estrogenic activity.[4]

This means they can disrupt your hormones and even alter the development of your cells, which puts infants and children at even greater risk. In this particular study, even HDPE products that were free of bisphenol-A (BPA) *still tested positive for other estrogenic chemicals.* **Use with caution.**

#3 – PVC (polyvinyl chloride)

PVC is used in plastic cooking oil bottles, deli and meat wrappers, shrink wrap, sandwich baggies, and plastic "saran" wrap. It is also found in plastic toys, lunch boxes, table cloths and blister packs used to hold medications. And it is commonly used to make jewelry and faux-leather purses, shoes and jackets.

PVC contains numerous toxic chemicals including lead and DEHP, a type of phthalate used as a plastics softener. As if the lead weren't bad enough, phthalates are considered "gender-bending" chemicals which cause the males of many species to become more female. These chemicals disrupt the endocrine systems of wildlife, causing testicular cancer, genital deformations, low sperm counts and infertility in a number of species, including polar bears, deer, whales, otters, and frogs, among others.

Scientists believe phthalates cause similar harmful effects in humans. If your home has flexible vinyl flooring, or those padded playmat floors for kids (often used in day cares and kindergartens, too), there's a good chance it is made from toxic PVC. PVC flooring has also been linked to chronic diseases like allergies, asthma and autism.

PVC is one of the worst health and environmental offenders. **Avoid at all costs.**

#4 – LDPE (low-density polyethylene)

LDPE is considered to be low-toxin plastic and it is used in bread bags, produce bags, squeezable bottles as well as coated paper milk cartons and hot/cold beverage cups. While LDPE does not contain BPA, it can leach estrogenic chemicals, much like HDPE. **Use with caution.**

#5 – PP (polypropylene)

Polypropylene is used in straws, yogurt containers, and syrup, ketchup, and medicine bottles. While polypropylene is considered a low-toxin plastic that is tolerant of heat, at least one study found that polypropylene plasticware used for laboratory studies did leach at least two chemicals.[5] **Use with caution.**

#6 – PS (polystyrene)

Polystyrene is also known colloquially as "Styrofoam," and is used in egg cartons, disposable plates, cups and bowls, take-out containers, coffee cups, meat trays, packing materials, and more. When heated, polystyrene can release *styrene*, a suspected nerve toxin and carcinogen.[6]

Heating styrofoam or using it for hot foods and beverages makes it leach toxins even more, so try to avoid food and drinks in polystyrene containers at all costs, and definitely don't use them in the microwave! **Avoid at all costs.**

#7 – Other

#7 is a catch-all designation used to describe products made from other plastic resins not described above, or those made from a combination of plastics. While there are many different types of #7 plastics, the most common include 5-gallon-size water bottles, baby bottles and other polycarbonate plastics.

It's difficult to know for sure what types of toxins may be in #7 plastics since they vary so much, but there's a very good chance that if they are polycarbonates, they contain bisphenol-A (BPA), or the equally concerning chemical created to replace BPA, known as Bisphenol-S (BPS).

BPA and BPS are both endocrine disrupters that interfere with your body's hormones, affecting your mood, growth and development, tissue function, metabolism, sexual function and ability to reproduce. Over 6 billion pounds of BPA are produced each year, so it is no wonder that the CDC found that **93% of Americans over the age of 6 have BPA in their urine and bloodstream!**[7]

Some of the greatest concern surrounds in-utero exposure to BPA and BPS, which can lead to chromosomal errors, spontaneous miscarriages and genetic damage.

But evidence is also very strong that these chemicals are harming adults and children, too, causing decreased sperm quality, early puberty, stimulation of mammary gland development, disrupted reproductive cycles and ovarian dysfunction, cancer, and heart disease.

Research has found that "higher BPA exposure is associated with general and central obesity in the general adult population of the United States."[8]

Another study found that BPA is associated not only with obesity, but also with insulin resistance, which is an underlying factor in many chronic diseases.[9] **Avoid at all costs.**

Plastic Harms the Environment

Plastics are not only an issue for our health, but also for the health of plants and animals everywhere.

In spite of nationwide recycling efforts, we currently recycle only a measly five percent of the plastics we produce. And *more and more cities are shutting down their plastic recycling programs because they are not cost effective!*[10]

Approximately 50 percent of our plastic waste goes to landfills (where it will sit for thousands of years due to limited oxygen and lack of microorganisms to break it down).

The remaining 45 percent ends up as litter in the environment where it ultimately washes out to sea, damaging marine ecosystems and entering the food chain. For example, 42% of the rivers tested in America turned up positive for Bisphenol-A or BPA.

According to Greenpeace, the world produces *200 billion pounds* of plastics every year. A whopping ten percent of that—or *20 billion pounds*—ends up in our oceans. Of that, about seventy percent sinks (Polycarbonate, Polystyrene, and PET), causing damage to the ocean floor.

The remaining 30 percent that floats (LDPE, HDPE, Polypropylene and foamed plastics) can be found all over the ocean, but eventually it all accumulates into massive, Texas-sized islands of floating trash called *gyres*. There are five of these enormous plastic islands floating and spiraling in the world's oceans today.

A United Nations report claims there is an average of **46,000 pieces of plastic in every square mile of ocean.**[11] Today, you can be aboard a ship thousands of miles away from land, but you will see floating plastic debris everywhere.

Even in the most remote reaches of the planet, you will find plastic trash. We've turned our oceans into the largest landfill in the world, and we should be ashamed!

The scariest part is that all those floating plastic particles act like "sponges" for waterborne contaminants such as PCBs, pesticides like DDT, herbicides, and other persistent organic pollutants. This makes floating plastics even more dangerous than they are on land.

Filter-feeding marine animals ingest these plastic particles and the toxins they contain, and subsequently pass them up through the food chain, and eventually to humans.

Scientists have not yet determined the full extent of the dangers posed by plastic consumption higher up the food chain, but we do know this: Fish and other sea creatures are being found with plastic in or around their bodies.

In fact, *forty-four percent* of all seabird species, 22 *percent* of Cetaceans (whales, dolphins and porpoises), **all** sea turtles, and a growing list of fish have been found to be contaminated with these materials.[12]

Tiny beads of plastic look like fish eggs or other food sources, so many sea creatures simply mistake them for food. Loggerhead sea turtles often confuse plastic bags with jellyfish, their favorite food. The effects of this are disastrous, including internal blockages, dehydration, starvation, and often, death.

Sea birds are frequently found strangled by the plastic rings that hold six-packs of soda together, or starved by stomachs full of plastic debris. Other creatures meet a painful end by getting tangled up in plastic netting.

Floating plastic debris also blocks the sunlight that sustains plankton and algae, and because plankton and algae are the foundation of the marine eco-system, this has an enormous effects up the food chain. *In some ocean waters, plastic outnumbers plankton by a factor of six to one.*

There is currently no feasible or affordable way to clean all the plastic out of the ocean. The ocean is far too violent and vast for that. The only thing we can do is clean up the beaches once all that plastic eventually washes up on them. (And because of natural ocean cycles, it eventually will.)

But if we want to really clean up our mess, the most effective, cheapest strategy is to prevent the plastic from getting there in the first place!

Plastic Pollution in the Air

According to the EPA, toxic pollutants, including styrene, butadiene and methanol are released into the air during the production of plastic—for all of us to inhale. And air pollution is an ongoing by-product of plastic products as they are made, filled, packaged and transported to consumers.

According to the National Resources Defense Council:

"In 2006, the equivalent of 2 billion half-liter bottles of water were shipped to U.S. ports, creating thousands of tons of global warming pollution and other air pollution. In New York City alone, the transportation of bottled water from western Europe released an estimated **3,800 tons** of global warming pollution into the atmosphere. In California, 18 million gallons of bottled water were shipped in from Fiji in 2006, producing about **2,500 tons** of global warming pollution."[13]

And that's just for bottled water!

From creation to disposal, plastic contributes significantly to air pollution, and many of the chemicals that go into their production continue to leach out into the air and into the food and beverages they hold.

Plastic Depletes Natural Resources

99% of all plastics are made from petroleum by-products. Every year, the oil used to produce just plastic water bottles in the U.S. alone is enough to fuel about 1,000,000 cars!

If you add in the oil used for everything else we make out of plastic, you can see the amount of oil wasted on stuff we throw away is simply astounding.

The more we squander what little accessible oil we have left on this planet on really stupid things like single-use plastic bottles, the more we have to procure from other countries and dangerously and expensively drill out of pristine ecosystems.

Given all the war, corruption and environmental devastation caused around the world by the demand for oil, this is neither politically nor environmentally sustainable. Anything we can do to quickly and permanently reduce our use of plastic would help improve our relationship with the people living in oil and gas-rich nations, reduce economic waste at home, and ease the huge burden that extracting fossil fuels places on communities and ecosystems worldwide.

20 Ways to Avoid the Toxins in Plastic

It is very possible to get most of the plastic out of your life, but it will take a little work. Start with the low hanging fruit first.

Here are some suggestions for reducing both your use of plastic and your exposure to its toxins:

1. Since plastic is found widely in processed food packaging (this includes canned foods and beverages, which have a plastic lining), the most profound thing you can do to reduce plastic toxins in your life is to **change your diet** to include primarily fresh, whole, unpackaged foods from the farmer's market or food co-op. Buying in bulk or joining a buying club can make this very affordable.

2. **Get your fresh eggs in cardboard cartons**, not polystyrene. Get your fresh meat and cheese

wrapped in waxed butcher paper, instead of plastic and foam. Get your fresh milk in bottles, not plastic-coated cartons or jugs. Many stores and farmers encourage you to return the empty bottle in exchange for savings on your next full one.

3. **Avoid canned foods and beverages**, including canned baby formulas. You can get many canned food items, like crushed tomatoes or broth, in glass jars or tetrapaks instead. A small handful of companies are offering their products in BPA-free cans, and the number continues to grow due to public demand.

4. When shopping, **use reusable mesh produce bags to hold your produce**, and reusable grocery bags to carry all your items home. You can also get reusable cotton sacks for bulk items like coffee, rice and nuts.

5. **Store, reheat or freeze your leftovers in glass containers** instead of in plastic "tupperware" or plastic wrap. Use reusable cloth baggies instead of plastic baggies for lunches and snacks. Use old-fashioned, waxed butcher paper to store meats and cheeses. Use reusable freezer bags to hold freezer items that can't go into glass or butcher paper.

6. **Use reusable glass or stainless steel water bottles** to carry water with you. Also bring your own stainless steel coffee thermos to the coffee shop or office with you. Most coffee shops have no problem putting your latté in a reusable thermos.

7. **Avoid disposable plastic or polystyrene dishes and utensils.** Instead, go to the thrift store and get a stack of super cheap mismatched ceramic dishes and stainless steel cutlery that you use only for parties, picnics and the like.

8. **Replace your plastic kitchenware** with items made from stainless steel, glass, ceramic, or even silicone instead.

9. **Bring your own containers to the restaurant** for both carryout and leftovers.

10. Ask for your newspaper and dry cleaning without plastic wrap.

11. **Don't take the receipt at the register,** or only handle it using gloves. Those slick, thermal-paper cash register receipts are a major source of BPA contamination via your skin.

12. **Get a good water filter for your tap**, and a reusable glass or steel bottle to replace plastic water bottles. Or, if you must buy bottled water, buy it only in reusable 5-gallon polycarbonate containers, and keep them in a cool, dark place.

13. **Make your own shampoo, lotions, liquid soaps, and cosmetics and store them in glass**, ceramic or stainless steel containers. There are tons of DIY recipes on the internet you can make to replace all the plastic bottles of personal care potions you currently use.

14. **Replace your toothbrush with a non-toxic one.**[14] Avoid plastic toothpaste tubes (and nasty chemicals too) by making your own toothpaste.

15. **Always ask for BPA-free dental sealants and BPA-free composite fillings** at the dentist office. If your dentist doesn't offer them, find one that does.

16. **Use cloth diapers.**

17. Because children are extra susceptible to the toxins in plastics, it is especially important

to **make sure your baby bottles, pacifiers, teething toys (or anything that ends up in your child's mouth) are safe.** Choose glass bottles with real rubber nipples, wood or cloth teethers, etc.

18. **Choose wood, cloth, steel and paper-based toys for your children** over plastic, whenever possible. This is especially important while your kids are still young enough to put things in their mouths. When they are older, see if you can get gently used plastic toys like Legos second hand from eBay, Craigslist or other online outlets.

19. **Replace your school-age child's plastic lunchbox** with a cloth or stainless steel one. There are many plastic-free lunchbox choices available, and most are great for adults, too!

20. **Make your own cleaners from non-toxic ingredients,** and store them in glass jars and bottles. You can even take the spray pump off of an old spray bottle, and screw it onto a recycled glass vinegar bottle.

Notes

1. http://news.discovery.com/human/health/are-bpa-alternatives-just-as-bad-130128.htm, http://www.ewg.org/enviroblog/2008/05/cheatsheet-phthalates, http://www.ewg.org/enviroblog/2008/04/cheatsheet-bisphenol-bpa

2. http://www.sciencedirect.com/science/article/pii/S0043135407005246

3. http://www.sciencedirect.com/science/article/pii/S0160412011002224

4. http://www.ncbi.nlm.nih.gov/pmc/?term=10.1289/ehp.1003220#Supplemental%20Material

5. http://www.ncbi.nlm.nih.gov/pubmed/18988846

6. http://www.sciencedirect.com/science/article/pii/S1001074207600709

7. http://www.cdc.gov/exposurereport/pdf/FourthReport_ExecutiveSummary.pdf

8. http://www.ncbi.nlm.nih.gov/pubmed/21676388

9. http://www.ncbi.nlm.nih.gov/pubmed/22090277

10. http://qz.com/117151/us-states-banned-from-exporting-their-trash-to-china-are-drowning-in-plastic/

11. http://www.unep.org/regionalseas/marinelitter/publications/docs/plastic_ocean_report.pdf

12. http://www.5gyres.org/the-plastic-problem/

13. http://www.nrdc.org/water/drinking/qbw.asp#environment

14. Find non-toxic toothbrushes here: http://thesoftlanding.com/bpa-pvc-and-phthalate-free-toothbrush-guide/

21.

Why You Should Start a Food Buying Club

Whether it is organic produce, non-toxic shampoos and deodorants, or a half-side of grass-fed beef, you and a group of your friends or associates can get together and order just about anything that can be had more cheaply by buying it in bulk.

Between rising food and oil prices and a depressed economy, organic, pasture-raised, and healthy, natural products are more expensive than ever. But you can make them *substantially cheaper* by throwing in with your friends and family to buy in larger quantities.

In the first study of its kind to look into the benefits of buying in bulk, research conducted by Portland State University Food Industry Leadership Center for the Bulk is Green Council (BIG), revealed that Americans could save an average of **89 percent** on costs by buying their organic foods in bulk.

Bulk foods obviously use far less packaging, but you may not realize how quickly this adds up.

According to the report, if Americans purchased the following products in bulk for one year, it would save *hundreds of millions* of pounds of waste from going into landfills:

- **Coffee:** 240 million pounds of foil packaging saved from landfills.

- **Almonds:** 72 million pounds of waste saved from landfills.

- **Peanut butter:** 7 pounds of waste saved from landfills *per family.*

- **Oatmeal:** Saves five times the waste of its packaged equivalent.

There are benefits to manufacturers too, who can save an average of 54 percent on material and delivery costs by packing foods like nuts, dried fruit and trail mix in bulk.

· ·

Even if you aren't in a buying club, buying in bulk at the grocery store is still a great way to save. Bring some reusable cotton drawstring bags to store your items in and avoid the toxic, wasteful plastic!

How to Start a Food Buying Club

If you have a large enough group to meet the minimum order price on a relatively regular basis, you can set up a wholesale account with a lot of different natural product and organic food vendors, both local and out-of-state. **This can save you hundreds—or even thousands of dollars a year!**

Some of the benefits of buying clubs include:

- Access to high-quality, natural and organic products at bulk or wholesale prices.

- Buying clubs build a sense of community amongst the members.

- Members gain a greater connection to their local small businesses, farms and ranches.

- Members share opinions and learn about products from each other.

- Buying in bulk also reduces the amount of packaging that is produced by the manufacturer.

- Reducing carbon emissions due to shipping only one order per club purchase vs. if members ordered individually.

- Purchasing products from businesses, farms and ranches that share similar values as your club.

Most companies that take wholesale orders have an order minimum. To meet that minimum, you usually need to start with just five or six families.

As word spreads, you will grow and soon you will need tools like Google Groups to communicate and Google Docs spreadsheets to place and keep track of orders among dozens of families.

Paypal or other electronic payment services may become invaluable for ensuring that members pay for their orders in a timely fashion.

Eventually, you will need some administrative leadership and some formal rules to keep everything organized and accountable. Whether the leadership is formal or informal, static or rotating, paid or voluntary depends on what works for your group.

Ultimately you will grow to need a food scale and a few used, deep-chest freezers (ideally bought second-hand, maybe from Craigslist) to hold orders in someone's garage until they can be picked up by members.

If you wanted to, you could grow so large that you need a storefront or warehouse to hold all the products. Indeed, most co-op grocery stores got their start as little garage-and-kitchen-table operations.

Between gardening, buying clubs and farmer's markets, you might barely need the grocery store anymore—and you certainly need never pay retail "Whole Paycheck" prices for expensive things like non-toxic sunscreen, organic flour or pasture-raised poultry.

And as an added benefit, you have the satisfaction of knowing that most of the money you spend on food, housewares and personal care is going to great small businesses and nearby family farms and ranches, instead of huge, unaccountable, corporate chains.

Once you get your buying club together, you'll be amazed at the deals you can negotiate simply by having a group large and organized enough to regularly buy in bulk.

· ·

You almost never have to buy a new freezer. There are simply too many used ones in perfect working condition to keep out of the landfill!
Try Craigslist or your local paper.

Natural Companies with Wholesale Pricing

The number of vendors offering great deals to buying clubs and co-ops grows every year. To get you started, here are just a few of the great national and regional vendors that cater to buying clubs or let you set up wholesale accounts:

AzureStandard.com - From organic cereals, pasta, and yogurt, to bulk nuts and produce, if it's a packaged food you've seen at a health food store, Azure probably has it. Only available in certain parts of the country.

FrontierCoop.com - Frontier is a national co-op that provides buying clubs with teas, coffees, spices, bulk food items, personal care items, household items, culinary accessories, vitamins, and supplements. They have thousands of Fair Trade items and carry all the major, natural brands like Frontier, Simply Organic, Aura Cacia, Ecover, Seventh Generation, Dr Bronner, and more.

BenefitYourLife.com - Natural and gluten-free foods, including bulk, unpasteurized, organic almond flower at the best 25-pound price I've seen anywhere.

MountainRoseHerbs.com - An outstanding source for any and every type of herb, spice, tea, essential oil or traditional fat you might need for cooking or natural medicine. Their vast selection can't be beat, and their prices are great, even at retail.

Working with a co-op to order wholesale is even better!

GreenPasture.org - Your grandmother was right: Cod liver oil is one of the most nutrient-dense foods you can add to your diet to ensure good health. If you ferment it in the old, Norwegian tradition the way Green Pastures does it, then it is even better.

WildernessFamilyNaturals.com - Sustainably harvested and produced coconut oils, coconut milk and cream, chocolate spreads and nut butters, sprouted nuts and seeds, soy- and canola-free mayonnaise and salad dressings, REAL wild rice, and more. One of my favorite traditional food stores!

AncientOrganics.com - Yummy ghee. Mmmmmm.

GreenVirginProducts.com - Bulk soap nuts and mineral salt deodorant stones.

Sheltons.com - Pasture-raised, antibiotic and hormone free chicken and turkey. West Coast only.

JandJGrassfedBeef.com - A grassfed beef CSA with yummy steaks and really nice ranchers. Southern California only.

GlacierGrown.com - Free-range bison by the half and whole animal (though butchered for easy sharing), raw honey. Southern California only.

You can also negotiate bulk orders from small businesses, farms and ranches in your town and around your county.

You can often find local:

- organic produce

- raw honey

- raw milk, butter and cheese (by the 5-pound block!)

- olives and olive oil

- pasture-raised pork

- grass-fed beef or bison

- pasture-raised chickens and eggs

- duck eggs

- fish and seafood

- diapers (both cloth and "eco-friendlier" disposables)
- hand-crafts

As a group, you can also go in together on online orders for clothing, housewares and more. You can start clothing or toy swaps among members, too.

Consider keeping a member business list so that you can hire *each other* for services before you open the Yellow Pages to hire a stranger.

Have everyone bring some food, and make your order pick-up days joyful, lively social occasions and multi-family playdates.

It's amazing how social, sustainable, frugal, and fulfilled you can be when you start working together and sharing resources with your friends and neighbors.

Starting or joining a natural food buying club this year just makes good economic and environmental sense. It can also help connect you with the farmers and food produced locally in your region, and build a strong sense of community and connection in your neighborhood, social group and family.

What do you have to lose?

. . . .

A well organized buying club can negotiate to buy just about anything at wholesale price or better. This includes organic food, diapers, clothing, furniture, and even appliances! Most retailers don't mind offering great discounts when you will be buying a large amount of their product.

Resources

1. A Cooperative Food-Buying Club Primer - http://www.vegfamily.com/articles/coop-food-buying.htm

2. Food Buying Clubs: Discount Prices for Organics and Building Community - http://www.organicconsumers.org/articles/article_3186.cfm

3. Bulk Is Green Council 2012 - http://www.bulkisgreen.org/Docs/2012-PSU-BIGStudy.pdf

22.

Save Hundreds on Food by Joining a CSA

Imagine coming home with a big box of seasonal produce every week, picked fresh and packed just for you.

This week, your box contains fresh strawberries, apricots, carrots, onions, mixed salad greens, mint, kale, spinach, broccoli greens, radishes, and beets, plus two new recipes to try.

The 100% organic food was picked yesterday, and *the whole box cost you **less than half** of what you would have paid for conventional produce at the grocery store.*

And yum, are those early strawberries sweet!

So how exactly do you get in on this deal?

What is Community Supported Agriculture?

Over the last 20 years, CSA or **Community Supported Agriculture** has become an increasingly popular way for people to buy local, seasonal—often organic—food directly from a farmer at a great price.

CSAs are popping up all over the country as the demand for local, farm-fresh food grows. These days, if you live within 100 miles of a farm, you probably live within 100 miles of a CSA!

The basics are simple: In a CSA, a farmer offers "shares" of farm produce for sale to the public. Interested buyers purchase a share, becoming CSA members, and in return receive a box (bag, basket) of seasonal produce harvested each week throughout the growing season.

This arrangement has many advantages for both the farmer and the buyer.

Farmers enjoy:

- Marketing the food early in the year, before the long days in the field begin

- Receiving payment early in the season, which the farmer needs cash flow the most

- Having an opportunity to get to know the people who eat the food they grow

- A higher return than is typical for selling produce to brokers, grocery stores or other wholesale outlets

CSA Members enjoy:

- Eating just-picked, local food, with *maximum flavor and vitamin content*

- Food that has less environmental impact because it was grown and sold locally

- Often lower cost for organic produce than at retail stores or even the farmer's market, while spending your money within your own community

- Exposure to new vegetables, new recipes, and new ways of cooking

- An opportunity to get to visit the farm at least once a season and sometimes socialize with other members.

- Developing a relationship with the farmer who grows their food and learning more about how food is grown

CSAs aren't confined to just produce. Some farmers also offer members shares of eggs, jam, homemade bread, meat, cheese, flowers or other farm products along with vegetables and fruit.

Sometimes, several farmers will offer their products together, to offer the widest variety to their members.

· ·

Find a CSA in your town by visiting LocalHarvest.org.

Building Local Food Communities

While the structure of a CSA is simple, there is an important concept woven into the CSA model that makes it a little different from the usual commercial transaction: the notion of **shared risk**.

Shared risk is part of what creates a sense of community among members, and between members and the farmers.

As a CSA shareholder, you have *a stake in the success of the farm*, so if a hailstorm takes out all the squash, everyone is disappointed together, and together you all rally for the tomatoes and peppers.

Most CSA farmers feel a great sense of responsibility to their members, and when certain crops are scarce, they make sure the CSA gets served first.

Still, very occasionally things go wrong on a farm—like they do in any kind of business.

If this potential makes you feel anxious, then the shared risk of a CSA may not be for you, and you should shop at your farmers' market.

LocalHarvest.org, a national non-profit connecting people with the small family farmers in their community, reports that they get complaint calls on between 2 and 9 CSA farms every year—*out of several thousand nationwide.*

Usually the cause of the complaint comes down to a failure to deliver as promised because of a catastrophic divorce, major illness, extreme weather, or a new farmer that got in over his or her head.

Sometimes, however, the CSA member simply did not do his or her due diligence and had unreasonable expectations.

Ultimately, nothing beats a personal conversation with the farmer. Here are the questions Local Harvest recommends you might ask before joining a CSA:

- How long have you been farming?

- How long have you been doing a CSA?

- Are there items in your box grown by other farms, and if so, which farms?

- How did last season go?

- How many members do you have?

- What percentage of the food you deliver annually is grown on your farm? If the answer is less than 100%, ask where the rest of the food comes from, whether it's certified organic (if that is important to you), and whether members are told which items come from off-farm.

- I'd like to talk with a couple of your members before I commit. Could you give me contact info for a couple of "references"?

Taking the time to check out your CSA farmer will help ensure a long-lasting and rewarding relationship between you, the farmer, your community and your food.

Local Acts with National Impact

Community Supported Agriculture is a simple idea, but its impact has been profound. Tens of thousands of families across the country have joined CSAs, and the numbers are growing exponentially every year. In some areas of the U.S., there is more demand for Community Supported Agriculture than there are farms to fill it!

In the burgeoning market for whole, organic food, CSA offers an outstanding way for new farmers, small farmers and even homesteaders to provide a secure, diversified living for themselves on a small parcel of land.

If CSA sounds like an ideal way to enjoy local, fresh produce to you, then LocalHarvest.org has the most comprehensive directory of CSA farms in the United States, with over **4,000 farms** listed in their database, so you can easily find and join a CSA in your community.

. . . .

Get some great tips for having a successful and rewarding CSA membership at www.localharvest.org/csa/tips.jsp.

23.

The High Cost of Food Waste

There are consequences to our national habit of sending food to landfills. American food waste has significant environmental, economic, and cultural ramifications.

On average, Americans waste a whopping **40 percent of our food supply**, which is **more than 1400 calories of food per person per day**, reports a study by a team of National Institute of Health researchers.[1]

The cost of food waste is $136 billion nationally, or about **$600 per household each year!**

In other words, the food we waste is more than enough to feed the *nearly 20% of Americans* experiencing food insecurity and hunger each year.[2]

According to **WastedFood.com**, wasting food squanders the time, energy, and resources—both money, soil and oil—used to produce that food. Increasingly, great amounts of fossil fuel are used to fertilize, apply pesticides to, harvest, and process food.

Still more gas is spent transporting food from farm to processor, wholesaler to restaurant, store to households, and finally to the landfill.

Food waste now accounts for more than one quarter of our total fresh water consumption and about 300 million barrels of oil per year!

All these expensive, precious resources are literally thrown away on managing food waste. *What on earth are we thinking?!*

And if that weren't enough, food rotting in landfills contributes to air pollution and global warming.[3] Landfills are America's *primary* source of methane emissions, and the second-largest component of landfills are organic materials that could be composted.

When food decomposes in a landfill, it releases methane, a greenhouse gas **21 times more damaging** than carbon dioxide. Furthermore, wet food waste is the main threat to groundwater or stream pollution in the event of a liner leak or large storm.

Food does NOT belong in landfills!

An Ounce of Prevention

Given the prevalence of food waste, what can we do to keep it out of landfills?

The Environmental Protection Agency provides a useful resource with its **Food Waste Recovery Hierarchy**.[4] At the top of the list is "source reduction," or, in laymen's terms, **buying less**.

That means making meal plans and shopping lists, and sticking to them. At restaurants, this means ordering sensibly and taking home leftovers.

Reducing waste also means buying locally produced food as much as possible.[5] If farmers have strong local demand for their products, and can deliver foods often fresh-picked the day before, there is naturally less spoilage and waste.

And with strong local farm markets and CSA programs, you are less likely to buy more than you need for the week.

Reduce Food Waste in Your Community

After source reduction, **feeding hungry people** through food recovery or gleaning is the next best way to curb food waste. Food-recovery groups rescue edible but unsalable food from supermarkets, restaurants, and institutional kitchens.

Gleaning is the practice of picking crops that a farmer plans to leave in the field. Whole fields are often left unharvested because the crop's market price won't justify the expense. This food should not go to waste as long as there are hungry families in our communities!

Feeding animals comes next in the hierarchy, so don't feel bad about slipping your scraps to Spot. On small farms, hogs, cows, chickens and other livestock were traditionally fed household food waste, and on a larger scale they could be fed commercial food waste today. Many small and mid-size farmers would be thrilled to reduce their feed costs while diverting food from landfills.

Fats and greases can be diverted to rendering plants that make soap. If you're brave enough, you can try rendering soap at home.[6]

Increasingly, used cooking oil is being used as a *fuel source* for diesel vehicles—a home chemistry process which, if you're brave enough, you can also try it at home.[7]

Another waste-to-energy scheme is **anaerobic digestion.** While it's not yet on the EPA's hierarchy, the process harnesses bacteria to convert food and yard waste into bio-gas that can power vehicles or create electricity.

Americans have long used the process to create energy from animal manure, but businesses on both coasts will soon use the process to transform supermarket and municipal food waste into power.

At the very least, food should be **composted.** Many individuals, schools, universities, hospitals, and municipalities have been doing so for years.

Composting costs roughly the same as regular waste collection and, depending on landfill tipping fees, can be even cheaper.

What comes at a high price, however, is wasting a resource like food by sending it to landfills.

When that happens, we squander the time, money, fertile topsoil, natural resources, and human effort that went into producing that item, while ignoring the environmental impact.

That's no way to sustain future generations!

Reducing Waste in Your Pantry

There are several ways to reduce food waste in your fridge and pantry.

First, plan your meals every week with shopping lists. Meal planning is one of the best ways to save money, time and effort in the kitchen, especially if you cook from scratch.

Can you imagine that this used to be taught in every home-ec class in the nation as part of responsible household stewardship?

If you aren't good at meal planning, there are recipe software programs to help you with that as well as many great meal plan apps and services available online.[8]

Second, do not store fruits and vegetables to-gether. Fruits that give off high levels of ethylene (the ripening agent) can prematurely ripen and spoil surrounding fruits and vegetables.

Third, consider purchasing products that can help extend the life of your fruits and veggies.

You can buy products that actually absorb ethylene and can be dropped into a crisper, such as the egg-shaped E.G.G. (for ethylene gas guardian), and the ExtraLife, a hockey puck-like disk.

A variety of produce bags are also on the market, like the Evert-Fresh and BioFresh, which both absorb ethylene and create an atmosphere that slows down decay. Be sure to wash and reuse them.

Best Food Storage Methods

- **Nuts and Seeds** - store nuts and seeds in jars in the refrigerator, especially if you have soaked and dried them for maximum nutrition first.[9]

- **Dried beans, whole grains and rice** - store in airtight, mouseproof containers. Recycle some of those silica dessicant packs you get in vitamin bottles into your container to absorb excess moisture.

- **Eggs** - if your eggs are fresh from the henhouse and never refrigerated, leave on your counter at room temperature for up to two weeks. Otherwise always refrigerate eggs.

- **Milk and cheese** - store in the fridge. If your milk is on the verge of going bad, you can culture it into yogurt or kefir, and it will last much longer.

- **Meats** - store in the fridge or freeze wrapped in waxed butcher paper. Smoking, salt curing, lactofermenting, and other methods of preserving meat are beyond the scope of this book, but worth checking out if you are into charcuterie.

VEGETABLES

- **Artichokes** - place in an airtight container sealed, with light moisture.

- **Asparagus** - place them loosely in a glass or bowl upright with water at room temperature. (Will keep for a week outside the fridge.)

- **Avocados** - place in a paper bag at room temp. To speed up their ripening- place an apple in the bag with them.

- **Arugula** - arugula, like lettuce, should not stay wet! Dunk in cold water and spin or lay flat to dry. Place dry arugula in an open container, wrapped with a dry towel to absorb any extra moisture.

- **Basil** - is difficult to store well. Basil does not like the cold, or to be wet for that matter. The best method here is an airtight container/jar loosely packed with a small damp piece of paper inside- left out on a cool counter.

- **Beans, shelling** - open container in the fridge, eat ASAP. Some recommend freezing them if not going to eat right away.

- **Beets** - cut the tops off to keep beets firm, (be sure to keep the greens!) Beets should be washed and kept in and open container with a wet towel on top.

- **Beet greens** - place in an airtight container with a little moisture.

- **Broccoli** - place in an open container in the fridge or wrap in a damp towel before placing in the fridge.

- **Broccoli Rabe** - left in an open container in the crisper, but best used as soon as possible.

- **Brussels Sprouts** - If bought on the stalk leave them on that stalk. Put the stalk in the fridge or leave it on a cold place. If they're bought loose store them in an open container with a damp towel on top.

- **Cabbage** - left out on a cool counter is fine up to a week, in the crisper otherwise. Peel off outer leaves if they start to wilt. Cabbage might begin to loose its moisture after a week , so, best used as soon as possible.

- **Carrots** - cut the tops off to keep them fresh longer. Place them in a closed container with plenty of moisture, either wrapped in a damp towel or immersed in water. They will stay crisp in the refrigerator for weeks. (Make sure to change the water frequently.)

- **Cauliflower**- will last a while in a closed container in the fridge, but they say cauliflower has the best flavor the day it's bought.

- **Celery** - does best when simply placed in a cup or bowl of shallow water on the counter.

- **Celery root/Celeriac** - wrap the root in a damp towel and place in the crisper.

- **Corn** - leave unhusked in an open container if you must, but corn really is best the day it's picked.

- **Cucumber** - wrapped in a moist towel in the fridge. If you're planning on eating them within a day or two after buying them they should be fine left out in a cool room.

- **Eggplant** - does fine left out in a cool room. Don't wash it, eggplant doesn't like any extra moisture around its leaves. For longer storage- place loose, in the crisper.

- **Fava beans** - place in an air tight container.

- **Fennel** - if used within a couple days after it's bought fennel can be left out on the counter, upright in a cup or bowl of water (like celery). If wanting to keep longer than a few days place in the fridge in a closed container with a little water.

...ic - store in a cool, dark, place.

Green garlic - an airtight container in the fridge or left out for a day or two is fine, best before dried out.

- **Greens** - remove any bands, twist ties, etc. most greens must be kept in a crisper or container with a damp cloth to keep them from drying out. Kale, collards, and chard even do well in a cup of water on the counter or fridge.

- **Green beans** - they like humidity, but not wetness. A damp cloth draped over an open or loosely closed container.

- **Green tomatoes** - store in a cool room away from the sun to keep them green and use quickly or they will begin to color.

- **Herbs** - keep in a closed container in the fridge for up to a week. Any longer might encourage mold. Alternatively, hang to dry in a cool, dark area.

- **Lettuce** - keep damp in an airtight container in the fridge.

- **Leeks** - leave in an open container in the crisper wrapped in a damp cloth or in a shallow cup of water on the counter (just so the very bottom of the stem has water).

- **Okra** - doesn't like humidity, so store in a dry towel in an airtight container. Doesn't store that well, best eaten quickly after purchase

- **Onion** - store in a cool, dark and dry place- good air circulation is best, so don't stack them.

- **Parsnips** - an open container in the crisper, or, like a carrot, wrapped in a damp cloth in the fridge.

- **Potatoes** - (like garlic and onions) store in cool, dark and dry place, such as, a box in a dark corner of the pantry; a paper bag also works well.

- **Radicchio** - place in the fridge in an open container with a damp cloth on top.

- **Radishes** - remove the greens (store separately) so they don't draw out excess moisture from the roots and place them in a open container in the fridge with a wet towel placed on top.

- **Rhubarb** - wrap in a damp towel and place in an open container in the refrigerator.

- **Rutabagas** - in an ideal situation a cool, dark, humid root cellar or a closed container in the crisper to keep their moisture in.

- **Snap peas** - refrigerate in an open container

- **Spinach** - store loose in an open container in the crisper, cool as soon as possible. Spinach loves to stay cold.

- **Spring onions** - Remove any band or tie and place in the crisper.

- **Summer squash** - does fine for a few days if left out on a cool counter, even after cut.

- **Sweet peppers** - Only wash them right before you plan on eating them as wetness decreases storage time. Store in a cool room to use in a couple a days, place in the crisper if longer storage needed.

- **Sweet potatoes** - Store in a cool, dark, well-ventilated place. Never refrigerate--sweet potatoes don't like the cold.

- **Tomatoes** - Never refrigerate. Depending on ripeness, tomatoes can stay for up to two weeks on the counter. To hasten ripeness place in a paper bag with an apple.

- **Turnips** - remove the greens (store separately) same as radishes and beets, store them in an open container with a moist cloth.

- **Winter squash** - store in a cool, dark, well ventilated place. Many growers say winter squashes get sweeter if they're stored for a week or so before eaten.

- **Zucchini** - does fine for a few days if left out on a cool counter, even after cut. Wrap in a cloth and refrigerate for longer storage.

FRUIT

- **Apples** - store on a cool counter or shelf for up to two weeks. For longer storage in a cardboard box in the fridge.

- **Citrus** - store in a cool place, with good airflow, never in an air-tight container.

- **Apricots** - on a cool counter to room temperature or fridge if fully ripe.

- **Cherries** -store in an airtight container. Don't wash cherries until ready to eat, any added moisture encourages mold.

- **Berries** - Don't forget, they're fragile. When storing be careful not to stack too many high, a single layer if possible. A paper bag works well, only wash before you plan on eating them.

- **Dates** - drier dates (like Deglet Noor) are fine stored out on the counter in a bowl or the paper bag they were bought in. Moist dates (like Medjool) need a bit of refrigeration if they're going to be stored over a week, either in cloth or a paper bag- as long as it's porous to keeping the moisture away from the skin of the dates.

- **Figs** - don't like humidity, so, no closed containers. A paper bag works to absorb excess moisture, but a plate works best in the fridge up to a week un-stacked.

- **Melons** - uncut in a cool dry place, out of the sun up to a couple weeks. Cut melons should be in the fridge, an open container is fine.

- **Nectarines** - (similar to apricots) store in the fridge is okay if ripe, but best taken out a day or two before you plan on eating them so they soften to room temperature.

- **Peaches** (and most stone fruit) - refrigerate only when fully ripe. More firm fruit will ripen on the counter.

- **Pears** - will keep for a few weeks on a cool counter, but fine in a paper bag. To hasten the ripening put an apple in with them.

- **Persimmon**
  –**Fuyu** - (shorter/pumpkin shaped): store at room temperature.
  –**Hachiya** - (longer/pointed end): room temperature until completely mushy. The astringentness of them only subsides when they are completely ripe. To hasten the ripening process place in a paper bag with a few apples for a week, check now and then, but don't stack-they get very fragile when really ripe.

- **Pomegranates** - keep up to a month stored on a cool counter.

- **Strawberries** - Don't like to be wet. Do best in a paper bag in the fridge for up to a week. Check the bag for moisture every other day.

* * *

Drop an ethylene gas absorber disk into your produce bin to greatly extend the life of your produce.

Notes

1. http://www.plosone.org/article/info:doi/10.1371/journal.pone.0007940

2. http://www.feedingamerica.org/hunger-in-america/our-research/hunger-in-america/

3. http://www.fao.org/docrep/018/i3347e/i3347e.pdf

4. http://www.epa.gov/wastes/conserve/smm/foodrecovery/

5. Why locally sourced food is important - http://www.smallfootprintfamily.com/why-eat-locally-grown-food

6. How to render soap - http://www.instructables. com/id/How-to-Make-Soap-3/step2/Obtain-Clean-Rendered-Fat/

7. How to make biodiesel - http://journeytoforever.org/ biodiesel_make.html#start

8. My favorite meal planning app - http://www. smallfootprintfamily.com/allergy-friendly-meal-plans

9. How to soak and dry nuts and seeds - http://www. smallfootprintfamily.com/why-you-should-soak-nuts-and-seeds

24.

How to Unclog a Drain Without Toxic Chemicals

When drains get clogged up, traditionally you have only a few choices: a plunger or drain snake that physically removes the clog, or some kind of caustic, toxic chemical like Drano.

Even a plumber will either use a plunger, snake or chemical to clear your drain. And they'll charge you a fortune to do it!

And while there is nothing wrong with using a snake or a **Zip-It** to clear your drains, chemical drain de-cloggers are highly toxic and go right into our waste-water stream where they are NOT properly filtered out, and eventually end up in our rivers and streams.

Drain Chemicals are Toxic to Everything

The main ingredients in chemical drain cleaners are **bleach** and **sodium hydroxide**, or NaOH, a highly corrosive salt.

Since NaOH is so corrosive, contact via inhalation, ingestion, skin, and the eyes can cause major irritation, vision problems, vomiting, shock if ingested, and even thermal and/or chemical burns.

Chronic exposure can cause nose and throat irritation, chest pains, dermatitis, and ulceration of the nasal passages. These effects are very severe and unfortunately much too common, as individuals do not heed the warnings and directions printed on the product's container.

Too often we reach for the dangerous stuff to get the job done, when there are usually safer and more natural ways to do the job.

So, to avoid using caustic chemicals, look no further than your kitchen pantry for everything you need to unclog a drain without causing damage to your health or the environment.

How to Unclog a Drain Naturally

Tools

- A cloth or rag, plunger or drain stopper to temporarily seal the drain.

- A tea kettle

Ingredients

- Small box of baking soda

- 1/2 cup vinegar

- 1 quart of water

Directions

1. Bail out any standing water in the sink until the sink and drain are relatively dry.

2. Dump about 1/2 of a box of dry baking soda down the drain.

3. Get your cloth or rags ready and at your side. You can also use a plunger or drain stopper for this, but be prepared to hold it down **tightly**.

4. Following the baking soda, pour 1/2 cup of vinegar down the drain.

5. **Immediately** after you pour it in, plug the drain with the cloth, rag or stopper, filling the drainhole completely so nothing can escape.

6. **HOLD TIGHT!** The interaction of the vinegar and baking soda will cause a "mini volcano" that will come up and out of the drain if you don't **keep it down there** to bust out your clog.

7. After the initial "volcano" subsides, leave the baking soda and vinegar mixture in the drain for about 30 minutes. While you are waiting, boil a tea kettle full of water.

8. After 30 minutes, remove the cloth or rag and **very slowly** pour the boiling water down the drain.

9. On the rare chance that your drain is not clear, just do it again.

How to Unclog a Toilet without a Plunger

1. As soon as you notice the toilet backing up, quickly remove the tank lid and close the flapper to prevent any more water from filling the bowl.

2. Add a few squirts of dishwashing liquid to a few cups of very hot water and carefully pour the mixture into the toilet bowl before you attempt plunging. You may not have to plunge at all.

Between a drain snake or Zip-It, and good old fashioned baking soda and vinegar, you can now unclog a drain very cheaply without dangerous chemicals, any time you need to!

25.

Recipes for a Green Clean

Approximately 85,000 chemicals are in use today. According to the Breast Cancer Fund, complete toxicological screening data is available for *only 7%* of these chemicals, and more than 90% have *never been tested for their effects on human health.* Wow!

According to the Environmental Protection Agency, household cleaning products rank among the most toxic everyday substances to which people are exposed, and most chemical brands are not safe.

Some especially toxic household cleaners include ammonia, chlorine bleach, aerosol propellants, detergents, petroleum distillates and toluene.

Many of these substances not only harm the skin, but they also give off toxic fumes that affect the person using the product and everyone else in the area.

Everything from dermatitis to headaches to cancer have been associated with the chemical products we use to clean our furniture, bathrooms and clothes, including air fresheners.

Traditional cleaning agents infect our lungs with carcinogens, assault our immune system, and expose us to unnecessary physical stress.

They are also typically made from petroleum, and remain toxic in the earth's soil, water, and environment for generations.

In contrast, green cleaning products are typically made with common kitchen ingredients like water, white vinegar, baking soda and castile soap. Some also include coconut or orange oils, and other powerful plant ingredients.

Making the switch to naturally derived, biodegradable, non-toxic cleaning products is easy. Today's green cleaning products have been proven to clean just as well—if not better than—traditional cleaning products without the side effects associated with the use of toxic chemicals.

As the health and environmental impacts of conventional cleaning products become more thoroughly understood, more and more brands of healthy, green, and effective cleaning products have started hitting the market. Look for brands like Branch Basics, Mrs. Meyer's, CitraSolv, Ecover, Seventh Generation, and Method next time you are at the store.

In these financially challenging times, being green usually means saving money too! These effective, non-toxic green cleaning recipes cost just pennies to make:

Homemade Glass Cleaner

Using isopropyl alcohol and white vinegar together makes a quickly evaporating spray glass and mirror cleaner that competes with national brands.

This formula can also be used to give a nice shine to hard tiles, chrome, and other surfaces.

If you use old newspaper to wipe your windows and mirrors, you'll have the ultimate eco-friendly, streak-free shine!

Ingredients

- 1 cup rubbing (isopropyl) alcohol

- 1 cup water

- 1 Tbsp. vinegar

Directions

1. Mix together in a reusable spray bottle.

All-Purpose Disinfectant

Use this spray to wipe down countertops, stovetops, toilets and other smooth surfaces

Ingredients

- 2 tsp. borax

- 1/4 cup vinegar

- 3-4 cups hot water

- 15 drops tea tree oil

Directions

1. Combine all ingredients in a spray bottle and mix well.

2. For extra cleaning power, add 1/4 tsp. liquid soap to the mixture.

Tub and Tile Scrub

Ingredients

- 1-2/3 cup baking soda

- 1/2 cup liquid soap

- 1/2 cup water

- 2 Tbsp. vinegar

Directions

1. Mix all ingredients, adding the vinegar after the other ingredients are well mixed. (if you add the

vinegar too early it will react with the baking soda).

2. Immediately apply, wipe and scrub.

Toilet Cleaner

Ingredients

- 1 cup of borax

- 1/4 cup vinegar

Directions

1. Pour both borax and vinegar into the toilet before going to bed. In the morning, scrub and flush.

Furniture Polish

Ingredients

- 1/4 cup olive oil

- 1/2 cup lemon juice

Directions

1. Mix into a bowl or spray bottle, and polish furniture with a soft cloth.

2. Wipe dry with another cloth.

Laundry Enhancers

To brighten laundry, add one half cup of strained lemon juice during the rinse cycle.

For a fabric rinse, add one quarter cup white vinegar during the washing machine's rinse cycle to remove detergent completely from clothes and soften them.

For more green cleaning recipes, my favorite book of genuinely effective homemade green cleaners is called *DIY Non-Toxic Cleaning Recipes* by Heather Dessinger (www.smallfootprintfamily.com/diy-non-toxic-cleaners).

Her Pink Grapefruit dishwasher powder is my favorite!

26.

Homemade Non-Toxic Laundry Detergent

These days, everyone is looking for ways to save some money. Fortunately for your wallet and the planet, the easiest way to save money in the laundry room is to make your own laundry detergent.

Making your own laundry detergent will not only save you money, but will naturally help you avoid the toxic chemicals and noxious scents found in store-bought brands.

Laundry detergent ingredients pose a variety of health risks to humans, ranging from relatively minor—like skin irritation and allergies—to the severe—cancer, poisoning and neurological problems.

These products can affect not only personal health, but also public and environmental health. The chemicals can go into the air, down the drain and into bodies of water, too.

. . . .

Wait till you have a full load before you wash your laundry. You'll save on water and heating costs, especially if you use cold water to rinse.

If you've ever wondered why your neighbor's "April Fresh" aroma gives you migraines, a 2008 University of Washington study of top-selling laundry products found that laundry products emitted **nearly 100 different volatile organic compounds.**[1]

Results of the study showed 58 different volatile organic compounds above a high concentration of 300 micrograms per cubic meter. Of these, seven are regulated as toxic or hazardous under federal laws.

All of the products tested in the study gave off at least one chemical regulated as toxic or hazardous, *but none of those chemicals was listed on the product labels.*

Findings in a 2011 study by the same researcher show that air vented from machines using the top-selling scented liquid laundry detergent and scented dryer sheet contains more than 25 volatile organic compounds, including *seven hazardous air pollutants.*[2]

Of those seven, two chemicals—acetaldehyde and benzene—are classified by the Environmental Protection Agency as known carcinogens, for which the agency has established **no safe exposure level.**

No wonder laundry products make an estimated 10% of the population feel so ill!

The researchers estimate that in the Seattle area, where the study was conducted, acetaldehyde emissions from the top five laundry detergent brands would constitute about 6 *percent* of automobiles' acetaldehyde emissions.

In the U.S. we regulate automobile emissions, but completely ignore the toxic pollution coming from our dryer vents—at our own peril.

. . . .

Add a 1/2 cup of vinegar to the rinse cycle of your washing machine to soften your clothes and save you from needing to buy a toxic chemical fabric softener or dryer sheet.

And if the toxic fragrances weren't enough, conventional laundry detergents also contain phosphates, sulfates, ammonia, naphthalene, phenol, optical brighteners, EDTA, and more.

These chemicals can cause rashes, itches, allergies, sinus problems, endocrine disruption, and have long term toxic effects on the environment.

Lastly, the embedded energy, natural resources and waste involved in mass-producing and transporting billions of gallons of plastic-packaged, toxic laundry detergents is just too significant for small footprint families to ignore.

Believe it or not, in the U.S., manufacturers are **not** required to list the ingredients used in laundry products, air fresheners and other household cleaning products.

Personal-care products often contain similar fragrance chemicals too, and although cosmetics are required by the Food and Drug Administration to list ingredients, no law requires products of any kind to list the chemicals used in fragrances and perfumes.

Even "green" or "eco-friendly" cleaning products are not required to disclose their ingredients, and may contain toxic fragrances or petroleum-derived ingredients.

The safest bet for your family and the planet is to make your own laundry detergent. Costing just *pennies* a load, you can get all the ingredients in bulk quantities online, at Costco, or in your grocer's laundry aisle.

Both the powder and liquid versions of this recipe work well in cold water and are safe for septic tanks, and both high-efficiency (HE) and front-loading washing machines.

I've found no difference in washing quality between the homemade detergent and store-bought brands, and this recipe tends to work *much better* than most eco-friendly brands.

··

Using non-toxic laundry detergent, vinegar as a fabric softener and then hanging your clothes to dry on a clothesline will give you the most affordable and planet-friendly laundry you can get!

For Cloth Diapers: If you want to use this detergent on cloth diapers, **you must omit the bar soap from the recipe.** Bar soap will build up on your diapers, repelling moisture, and eventually need stripping out.

Instead, wash your diapers in a combination of borax, washing soda and baking soda in the recipe below, with a vinegar rinse.

Homemade Laundry Detergent Powder

Makes about 200 loads

Tools

- Dust mask or bandana

- Gloves of some sort (dish, latex, gardening, etc.)

Ingredients

- 4 cups Borax

- 4 cups Washing soda

- 2 cups Baking soda

- 4 cups grated bar soap (2-4 bars) (*Choose a non-toxic, real bar soap—not a "beauty bar" like Dove or a clear glycerine soap. We use both Kirk's Castile and Grandma's Lye soaps for laundry.* **Omit for cloth diapers.***)*

- Essential oil (*Optional for scent. Tea Tree oil is especially nice if you use this detergent for washing cloth diapers.*)

Directions

1. Cut the bar soap into large chunks with a knife.

2. Grate the soap chunks with a fine cheese grater or throw the chunks into the food processor and blend into as fine of a powder as you can make. (*Put on your dust mask and let dust settle before opening processor, so as not to inhale it.*)

3. Put on your gloves and dust mask or bandana.

4. In a large plastic tub or bucket, mix the Borax, washing soda, and baking soda together. (*Washing soda and borax are skin irritants, so wear gloves. Wear a dusk mask or bandana to avoid breathing in the dry ingredients while you mix. You will need to let the dust settle a few times before continuing to stir. If you can seal the container, you can shake it vigorously to mix with no dust.*)

5. Stir in the grated/powdered bar soap.

6. Stir in 10-20 drops of essential oil, if tolerated. Tea tree oil is great for diapers as it has antiseptic qualities.

7. Store in a covered, airtight container.

8. If your powder has trouble completely dissolving, try mixing it in a little hot water before adding to the laundry.

9. Use 1-2 Tablespoons per load. (Adjust for your machine.)

Homemade Laundry Detergent Liquid

Makes enough for about 80 loads

Tools

- Dust mask or bandana

- Gloves of some sort (dish, latex, gardening, etc.)

- Hot water

- Clean 5-gallon bucket with lid

Ingredients

- 1 cup Borax

- 1 cup Washing soda

- 1/2 cup Baking soda

- 1 cup grated bar soap (1-2 bars) (*Choose a non-toxic, real bar soap. Do not use a "beauty bar" like Dove or a clear glycerine soap! We use both Kirk's Castile and Grandma's Lye soaps for laundry.* **Omit for cloth diapers.***)*

- Essential oil *(Optional for scent. Tea Tree oil is especially nice if you use this detergent for washing cloth diapers.)*

Directions

1. Cut the bar soap into large chunks with a knife.

2. Grate the soap chunks with a fine cheese grater or throw the chunks into the food processor and blend into as fine of a powder as you can make. Wear your dust mask or bandana, and let dust settle before opening processor, so as not to inhale it.

3. Place grated bar soap in a pot. Cover with water and simmer over medium heat until all soap is melted, stirring occasionally.

4. Pour melted soap mixture into a clean 5-gallon bucket.

5. Put on your gloves and dust mask or bandana.

6. Add washing soda, baking soda, and borax to the soap mixture and stir. *(Washing soda and*

*borax are skin irritants, so wear gloves. Wear a
dusk mask or bandana to avoid breathing in the
dry ingredients while you mix.)*

7. Add enough hot water to almost fill the
   bucket. Mix very well until all ingredients are
   dissolved. *(I use a long ruler for this.)*

8. If using essential oil, AFTER the mix has cooled
   down completely, mix in 10-20 drops, to taste.

9. Let sit overnight to gel. The gel will be loose
   and very gloppy—like egg-drop soup.

10. Use a funnel to pour the gel into clean,
    recycled detergent containers or leave in the
    bucket. Cover with an airtight lid if leaving in
    the bucket to protect children and pets.

11. Stir or shake well before using. Use 1/2 – 1 cup
    per load. (Adjust for your machine.)

Many do-it-yourself laundry detergent recipes call for Fels-Naptha, Octagon or Zote bar soap, which contain toxic ingredients and fragrances that you really don't want near your skin or in your environment. Choose a natural lye or castile soap instead.

A Word About Borax

Many people are concerned about whether borax is a safe chemical. There are many sites on the internet claiming it is toxic. I disagree with these sites and believe that borax is as safe as table salt or washing soda—in other words, *the dose makes the poison.*

Boron is an **essential trace mineral nutrient** important for many functions in the body, like metabolizing calcium and magnesium, rebuilding bones and teeth, hormone regulation, and maintaining communication between your cells.

In fact, boron is for the parathyroid gland what iodine is for the thyroid.

Boron is ubiquitous in soil and water, and is required for plant growth. Diets with a fair amount of fruit and vegetables provide about 2 to 5 mg of boron per day, but this also depends on the region where the food was grown and how it was grown.

Humans have mined and used borax since its discovery in Persia more than 4,000 years ago. Borax is a naturally occurring mineral found in dried salt lake beds, and consists of water, sodium, boron and oxygen. That's it!

All of the studies that showed evidence of possible hormone disruption in rats used *ridiculously* high doses of borax (many grams delivered intravenously).

The reason it has this effect at high doses is not because it is borax; it is because it is essentially an overdose of the element boron, which is a nutrient required for hormone regulation in small quantities.

Iron and calcium are required by the body too, but an overdose of either will also harm you.

However, people could never willingly ingest anything even close to the amount of borax required to do harm—unless they worked unprotected for years in a borax mine or packaging factory.

(Note: You will want to keep your small children out of the borax, just as you would keep them away from the vitamins, etc.)

Borax is classified as **non-carcinogenic** and a mild skin irritant. The high alkalinity of borax is what causes skin irritation, which is the same reason that washing soda and even baking soda cause skin irritation, too.

The alkaline pH of borax, washing soda and baking soda is what softens the water, and makes it possible for them to clean your clothes.

There are also several studies in the ToxNet database[3] that show borax is only a very mild lung irritant and causes no lasting damage. It is quickly excreted in the urine. In addition, it does not penetrate the skin well, and is not considered to be bio-accumulative.

Finally, the Material Safety Data Sheet[4] lists borax as a health hazard of 1, the same as baking soda and salt. In other words, borax is toxic in the same way that salt is toxic[5]: *A small amount can do great things; a huge amount will kill you and other living things.*

Borax is used in laundry detergents, hair potions and skin lotions. Like diatomaceous earth, it also can help kill fleas and dust mites in your carpet by dehydrating them. It is also used in safer ant and cockroach poisons.

Borax is also naturally anti-fungal and anti-viral (but not anti-bacterial), and—here's the neatest part—through a chemical reaction with water, borax produces hydrogen peroxide (the main ingredient in OxyClean) to brighten and sanitize your clothes.

Some people even ingest it mixed in water to self-treat various health conditions[6] that supplemental boron can really help, like arthritis, prostate cancer, fluoride detoxification, menopausal symptoms, psoriasis, and candida.

People should use the same precautions (gloves, dust mask or bandana) with borax that they would use around any dusty substance, like washing soda, bentonite clay, diatomaceous earth, or powdered soap. (*Heck, you don't even want to inhale flour or powdered sugar either for that matter!*)

In sum, borax is wholly natural. It doesn't cause cancer, accumulate in the body, or absorb through the skin.

Because the dose makes the poison, borax is not harmful to the environment any more than salt or washing soda is. In fact, the largest borax (borate) mine in the world—found in Boron, California—is considered by many to be the most ecologically sound and environmentally sustainable mine in the United States.

I consider borax a safe, effective cleaner that I will continue to use in my green cleaning and safer pest control.

Notes

1. http://www.sciencedaily.com/ releases/2008/07/080723134438.htm

2. http://www.sciencedaily.com/ releases/2011/08/110824091537.htm

3. http://toxnet.nlm.nih.gov/cgi-bin/sis/search2/f?./
   temp/~EIBkaj:3

4. http://www.sciencelab.com/msds.
   php?msdsId=9924967

5. http://www.sciencelab.com/msds.
   php?msdsId=9927593

6. http://www.health-science-spirit.com/borax.htm

27.

Homemade Fluoride-Free Toothpaste

Ever wonder why most kids' toothpastes have no fluoride?

Because kids will inevitably swallow some paste, and fluoride is extremely TOXIC. In fact, eating a tube of toothpaste will *kill* a child (and seriously harm an adult), so be sure to keep any fluoride paste or mouthwash out of reach of little ones, just like you do with bathroom cleaners and medicines.

For me, this begs the question:

> *Why are we putting a toxic chemical that every-one agrees should not be swallowed into our food and water supply in the first place?*

Most people don't know that the type of fluoride added to water supplies, some toothpastes, and many beverages and foods is not medical grade in the least. Rather it is a *waste product* of the nuclear, aluminum, and phosphate (fertilizer) in-dustries.

The EPA has classified fluoride as a toxin. Fluoride is so toxic that, in addition to being a primary, active ingredient in rat and cockroach poisons, pest fumigants and crop pesticides, fluoride is also an active ingredient in anesthetic, hypnotic, and psychiatric drugs, as well as nerve gas used by the military.

Under the U.S. Safe Water Drinking Act[1], it is ille-gal to dump fluoride in lakes, streams and oceans, but, for some strange reason, it's OK to dump fluo-ride into our food and water supplies and then rub it into our teeth and gums twice a day.

Do we really want this stuff inside our bodies at all, especially when there are non-toxic alternatives that work just as well?

. . . .

The American Academy of Pediatrics and the American Dental Association recommend you do NOT give fluoridated tap water to babies, or use it to make formula.

Fluoridation Is Not Effective

You might be worried about how removing fluoride from our drinking water or toothpaste might affect our teeth, but you needn't be.

While *topically-applied* fluoride can help prevent tooth decay in people who eat a diet high in sugar and processed foods, all of the recent large-scale studies of *water fluoridation* have shown that there are no proven, positive effects from the practice.[2]

None. No proof.

But there is plenty of proof of harm, including dental fluorosis, osteoporosis and bone scarring, brain tumors, fluoroderma, and more.[3] In fact, a recent Harvard study found that fluoride exposure can impair the neurological development of children![4]

According to statistics from the World Health Organization, the tooth decay rates of countries which do *not* fluoridate their water supplies are just as low, or even lower, than those countries which do.

Furthermore, several studies published since 2000 have reported that there has been no increase in tooth decay rates noted in communities which ended water fluoridation.

Fluoridation is illegal, banned or just not used in an overwhelming number of countries, including most industrialized countries.[5]

Despite pressure from the dental industry, 97% of continental western Europe has rejected, banned, or stopped fluoridation due to environmental, health, legal, or ethical concerns.[6]

And yet, their children's teeth are just as healthy as children's teeth in the U.S! In fact, in many parts of Europe where traditional, whole food diets prevail, they are healthier.

The good news is that the voice of concerned, unbiased science is beginning to overwhelm all the pro-fluoride industry propaganda.

For example, in November 2006, **the American Dental Association advised parents to avoid giving fluoridated water to babies or using it to make formula.**

Take the advice, and protect yourself and your children by avoiding the consumption of fluoride.

Here's more information about the dangers of fluoride and how to keep your teeth healthy without it, *possibly saving you a ton in dental bills*:

- **The Case Against Water Fluoridation** - (www. smallfootprintfamily.com/dangers-of-water-fluoridation) - The not-so-nice history of fluoridation, health problems caused or worsened by fluoride, and how to reduce your exposure from the many unexpected sources of fluoride in your life.

- *The Real Cause of Tooth Decay (and How to Stop it Naturally)* - (www.smallfootprintfamily.com/how-to-stop-tooth-decay) - What really causes cavities? It's not what you think! Can you heal a small cavity without a filling? Yes!

This is our family recipe for fluoride-free toothpaste. It helps remove stains, leaves a fresh feeling in the mouth, helps relieve sensitive teeth, and saves money too.

Homemade No-Fluoride Toothpaste

Ingredients

- 3 Tbsp. baking soda (mild abrasive)

- 1 Tbsp. finely ground sea salt *(mild antibacterial, whitener and good for the gums)*

- A few drops peppermint, spearmint, anise, clove or cinnamon bark essential oil, according to the taste you want *(be sparing, they are very strong)*

- 1 tsp. xylitol or a few drops of liquid stevia *(Optional but highly recommended; xylitol helps prevent tooth decay naturally)*

- 1/2 tsp. finely ground dried sage (*Optional; sage is antimicrobial, but it has a strong taste*)

- Organic virgin coconut oil, softened but not liquified (*Coconut oil is highly anti-microbial and also buffers the more abrasive ingredients.*)

Directions

1. Grind sea salt in a small coffee grinder, if needed, to make as powdery as possible.

2. Mix all ingredients except the coconut oil to taste. You can stop at this stage and use this as a tooth powder if you wish.

3. Mix in a teaspoon of coconut oil at a time until you find the right consistency for your paste.

4. Put into a small, resealable jar or squeezable container and keep in a relatively cool place.

5. Brush.

6. Don't forget to floss!

If you still have doubts, check out this movie from the Environmental Working Group (youtu.be/ St0VCXYTGcc) that expertly sums up how and why to avoid fluoride wherever you can.

Notes

1. http://water.epa.gov/lawsregs/rulesregs/sdwa/index. cfm

2. http://www.holisticmed.com/fluoride/nobenefit.html

3. http://www.fluoridealert.org/issues/health/

4. http://www.hsph.harvard.edu/news/features/ fluoride-childrens-health-grandjean-choi/

5. http://www.fluoridation.com/c-country.htm

6. http://www.fluoridealert.org/content/water_europe/

28.

Five Green Ways to Save on Baby Stuff

It is common for parents to complain about how much it costs to have a baby: how expensive all the things you supposedly need are, not to mention the hospital costs of labor and delivery, especially now that the U.S. has the highest cesarean rate in the world.

Fortunately, you don't have to believe the Baby Industry hype. It is possible to save hundreds—*if not thousands*—of dollars, and untold environmental resources by parenting closer to nature.

Here are five ideas to help you save money on baby.

Consider a Homebirth

If you are a low-risk pregnancy, and if you prefer to have a natural childbirth without pharmaceuticals, homebirth is a safe, low-tech, eco-friendly and in-expensive way to have a baby.[1] In fact, for low-risk women, homebirth is just as safe as hospital birth.[2]

The average uncomplicated vaginal birth costs **68% less** in a home than in a hospital, and births initi-ated in the home offer a lower combined rate of intrapartum and neonatal mortality, and a lower incidence of cesarean delivery.[3]

Not only do you get to relax and bring your pre-cious one into the world in the comfort of your own home, but you help conserve all of the gas, electricity, chemicals, and other expensive re-sources that go into a "high-tech," hospital birth.

Generally, all prenatal care (including lab tests and *hour-long* check-ups), post-natal care, and the birth itself can cost a mere $2,500-$5000, which is less than most people's out-of-pocket deductible ex-pense and co-pay for a hospital birth.

Some insurance companies will even reimburse for birth at home or at a birthing center.

Compare that to the national average cost of a hospital birth with no complications: $15,000! And if there are complications (which happen more often when hospitals use pitocin to speed labor), you could be looking at upwards of $30,000 for giving birth.

Savings: $7,500 and up

Breast Really is Best

Controversy notwithstanding, the science *is* definitive: breastfeeding is *far and away* better than formula feeding. While not every new mother is physically capable of breastfeeding, the vast majority of American mothers can, especially with the support of family and a lactation counselor.

Breastfeeding is considered so essential to the health of a mother and her baby that the American Academy of Pediatrics recommends breastfeeding for at least a year, and the World Health Association recommends at least 2 years. For non-Western cultures, the average length of breastfeeding is 4 *years!*

Formula feeding increases the risk of Sudden Infant Death Syndrome (SIDS) as well as diabetes, leukemia and several other diseases, costing us all a minimum of $3.6 billion dollars a year in health-care costs.[4]

The AAP says each formula-fed infant costs the healthcare system between $331 and $475 more than a breastfed baby in its first year of life. The cost of treating respiratory viruses resulting from not breastfeeding is $225 million a year.[5]

For the national Special Supplemental Nutrition Program for Women, Infants and Children (WIC), supporting a breastfeeding mother costs about 45 percent less than a formula-feeding mother. Every year, **$578 million** in taxpayer funds buys formula for babies who could be breastfeeding.[6,7]

Formula is not only substandard to breastmilk nutritionally, but its manufacture is also extremely resource intensive and toxic to the environment—even the organic brands.

An entire industrial complex goes into making commercial formula. After all, formula is *the epitome of processed food.*

The farming required to make formula requires vast tracts of land ravaged by the monoculture of genetically-modified (GMO) corn and soybeans, heavy machinery, synthetic fertilizers made from petroleum, toxic pesticides, and more.

And if that weren't enough, a recent study showed that 1 in 3 cans of infant formula *(including organic brands)* contained enough BPA in a single serving to expose an infant to BPA levels **more than 200 times** the government's safe level of exposure for the industrial chemical![8]

Lastly, formula feeding is extremely expensive for families. It costs between $700-$3000 a year to feed a baby with formula, and the organic formulas may even cost more.

While some may view this as the cost of convenience, I would argue that as a society, we can and should make it *much easier and more acceptable* for moms to breastfeed and/or pump their milk during the first years of their babies' lives.

And because there are families who simply cannot breastfeed, we also need to have safe, secure donor *Milk Banks* in every town so that nature's perfect infant food is available to *all* babies.

And, in a pinch, we need to make *whole food* formula recipes available to anyone who needs them. Our economy, our health and our environment depend on it. (See notes for recipes.[9])

That said, if you are able to breastfeed, choosing to do so for at least a year could save you enough money for a nice vacation after you wean.

Savings: $3,000

Skip the Nursery

Why does a baby need her own room and furniture, other than for the parent's entertainment value? When you think about it, what does a baby care about whether the bumper and the lamp match the blankets?

After all, what your baby really wants is to feel safe and be close to her parents. And all parents want is to know baby is safe, and to get a good night's sleep.

Many parents are asking this question and deciding to co-sleep with their child—skipping the cost of a nursery.

When you co-sleep, you don't need to buy a changing table, baby dresser or any of the furniture and decorations that would go into a nursery that your baby will only use for two short years, and never remember.

Co-sleeping with parents or grandparents is common practice throughout much of the world, and this saves a lot of natural resources, and a lot of money—which you can put into a big, king-size family bed!

Since babies and small children are evolutionarily wired to naturally fear being alone at night[10], having your child sleeping close to you means more restful nights for everyone.

By learning to safely co-sleep (See cosleeping.org), not only do you not have to get up at night repeatedly to feed baby, but your baby is more likely to sleep soundly without needing "training." As an added bonus, each day can begin with snuggles and smiles even before you get out of bed!

In fact, most kids don't need their own rooms or furniture until they are old enough for the Big-Kid Bed, at which point you can transition your child to the furniture that will last his or her entire life at home.

While some families choose to create a family bed, you could just as easily buy a sidecar co-sleeper or remove one of the sides of your crib and push it up against the bed. You can also lay a child's mattress on the floor next to your own.

Whatever you choose, baby will be close at hand, and you will need less space in your home, as well as save lots of money and natural resources.

Savings: $1,500 and up

Reduce, Reuse, Recycle

The Baby Industry makes a fortune on the fact that baby clothes and toys are relatively cheap and will only be worn or played with for a short time before they are outgrown.

That every family feels compelled to buy such quickly obsolete products like baby clothes, furniture and toys again and again may line the pockets of CEOs, but on a massive, nationwide scale, it is completely and totally **unsustainable**.

Consider buying your baby furniture, toys and clothes at thrift stores, E-Bay or CraigsList. Join sites like Toyswap.com or BabyPlays.com to get great used toys.

Check in your community for baby clothes swaps. Ask your friends and relatives for hand-me-downs.

Used clothing is not only eco-friendly and cheaper, but the neurotoxic, fire-retardant chemicals they put into many baby clothes (especially pajamas!) will have most likely been washed out already, making them a safer option for your little one.

Once you start asking around, you'll probably find that *most parents* of older kids have some old baby stuff stored away they'd love to sell or give away.

Savings: $300 and up

Cloth Diaper or Go Diaper Free

The average baby goes through 6-8 diapers a day. Unless you practice elimination communication (See diaperfreebaby.org.), your baby will use between **6,500–10,000 diapers** before potty training around 30 months old.

If you use disposables and disposable wipes, this can cost about $75–$100 a month retail—*at least $3,000 per child!*

We, as a nation, also pay *through the nose* for disposable diapers throughout their life-cycle. In the full-cost accounting, from **farm to factory to storefront**, compared to cloth diapers, disposables:

- create 2.3 times more water waste,

- use 3.5 times more energy,

- use 8.3 times more non-renewable raw materials (like oil and minerals),

- use 90 times more renewable raw materials (like tree pulp and cotton),

- and use 4 to 30 times as much land for growing or mining raw materials.

And these numbers account for the need to wash cloth diapers!

For the nation, this means that **over 250,000 trees** are destroyed and over **3.4 billion gallons of oil** are used *every single year* just to manufacture disposable diapers in the United States.

For that amount of oil, we could have powered over 5,222,000 cars in the same time period.

In contrast, reusable cloth diapers offer a solution to the cost, and all the health and environmental problems with disposables.[11] Today's cloth diapers are as effective as any disposable, and they come in lots of styles, sizes and super-cute colors and prints!

The new cloth diaper systems do not require a stinky diaper pail, and clean up easily in both regular and high-efficiency washing machines, *using less water than you would need to flush the toilet each time your baby went to the bathroom.*

A good cloth diapering system consisting of at least 24-36 cloth diapers will usually cost you between $200-500 dollars up front retail (even less second-hand), but you will not need to continue to buy them, and you can save them for use with future children.

That's **huge savings** over disposables!

And, if you thought using cloth diapers was natural, economical and environmentally friendly, imagine this prospect: ***not using any diapers at all!***

Throughout most of human existence, parents have kept their babies clean, dry and happy *without* using diapers.

And today, in many cultures around the world, mothers continue to practice some form of elimination communication (EC), where they learn their babies' cues for needing to eliminate—just as they would learn their cues for hunger or sleepiness—and hold them over a potty when they need to go.

Learning EC with your child can save you a fortune in diapers of any kind, and as an added bonus, your child will be fully potty-learned by age two!

Savings: $2500 and up

Total savings: At least $14,800

That's a ton of money saved, simply by opting out of the wasteful consumer status quo!

Notes

1. http://onlinelibrary.wiley.com/doi/10.1111/jmwh.12172/abstract

2.   *"Home births 'as safe as hospital"*, BBC News, April 15, 2009, http://news.bbc.co.uk/2/hi/health/7998417.stm.

3.   "The Cost-Effectiveness of Home Birth." J Nurse Midwifery. 1999 Jan-Feb;44(1):30-5.

4.   Jon Weimer, "The Economic Benefits of Breastfeeding: A Review and Analysis," Food and Rural Economics Division, Economic Research Service, U.S. Department of Agriculture, *Food Assistance and Nutrition Research Report* 13. (March 2001): 1-4.

5.   Lawrence M. Gartner, Arthur I. Eidelman, "Breastfeeding and the Use of Human Milk," American Academy of Pediatrics Policy Statement, Organizational Principles to Guide and Define the Child Health Care System and/or Improve the Health of All Children.

6.   Thomas M. Ball, Anne L. Wright, "Health Care Costs of Formula-feeding in the First Year of Life," *Pediatrics* 103, (4 April 1999): 870-876.

7.   "Over 101 Reasons to Breastfeed," Leslie Burby, 2007. An outstandingly well-researched and footnoted article.

8.   http://www.ewg.org/research/bisphenol

9.   Formula recipes - http://www.westonaprice.org/childrens-health/recipes-for-homemade-baby-formula

10. http://www.psychologytoday.com/blog/
freedom-learn/201110/why-young-children-protest-
bedtime-evolutionary-mismatch

11. Dangers of disposable diapers - http://www.
smallfootprintfamily.com/dangers-of-disposable-
diapers

29.

12 Ways to Celebrate an Eco-Friendly Holiday

Between Thanksgiving and New Year's Day, Americans throw away a million extra tons of garbage each week[1], including holiday wrapping and packaging.

All this waste is really unnecessary. Here are twelve eco-friendly holiday tips to help you reduce your environmental footprint this holiday season.

1. Make Your Own Wrapping Paper or Go Without

Most mass-produced wrapping paper you find in stores is not recyclable because of the shiny coatings, foils and colors, and therefore ends up in landfills.

And sadly, most wrapping paper and ribbon is produced in Asian sweatshops!

What a shame so many trees and oil are wasted every year solely to produce something that exists only to be torn off and thrown away!

Instead, here's a great chance to get creative! Wrap presents with old maps, the comics section of a newspaper, or children's artwork. Or use a scarf, attractive dish towel, bandana, or some other useful cloth item that is a gift in and of itself.

You could even go without wrapping your gifts altogether. A Small Footprint Family Facebook fan recently told me that at her home, she hides all the unwrapped presents around the house, and holds a scavenger hunt for the kids to find them.

What a fun, clever, low-waste idea!

2. Buy Energy-Saving Holiday Lights

Thanks to technology, you can now decorate your house with LED lights that use 90 percent less energy than conventional holiday lights, and can save your family up to $50 on your energy bills during the holiday season!

As an added bonus, LEDs release little heat, and they last about 200,000 hours. In the unlikely event that one does burn out, the rest of the lights keep on glowing.

Whew!

According to one U.S. Department of Energy study, if everyone replaced their conventional holiday light strings with LEDs, at least two billion kilowatt-hours of electricity could be saved in a month.

The savings would be enough to power 200,000 homes for a year!

LED lights are available online and at many major retailers.

3. Add Organic and Local Foods to Your Holiday Feast

Support local family farmers who grow sustainable meat and produce.[2] Not only does local, organic food taste better, but you'll also be doing your part for your community and the planet too.

Find an organic turkey or humane ham and local vegetables for holiday dinner at eatwild.com.

··

Instead of wrapping gifts, hide all the unwrapped presents around the house, and hold a scavenger hunt for the kids to find them.

4. Get a Pesticide-Free Tree

Demand is on the rise for Christmas trees that are not covered in chemicals. Some growers use 40 different pesticides, as well as chemical colorants.

The good news is that there are now a number of tree-farms that sell pesticide-free trees, so ask your local Christmas tree seller, or search for an organic tree farm near you.[3]

An even more eco-friendly option is to get a plant-able tree that you can put in the ground in your yard or a nearby park when you are done.

5. Recycle Your Christmas Tree

Each year, 10 million Christmas trees end up in the landfill. While your tree won't fit in the recycling bin with your newspapers and bottles, you can recycle your tree.

Many cities offer programs to turn your tree to mulch or wood chips. Some cities even use your old trees to do important environmental projects like streambank stabilization.

Visit the National Christmas Tree Association or do a search to find the tree-recycling program near you.[4]

6. Recycle Your Old Cellphone

Getting a new cell phone for Christmas? Not sure what to do with the old one?

Now, you can drop off that old phone at any Staples store, as part of the Sierra Club cell phone recycling program or possibly sell it to one of the many cell phone buyback programs online.

Each year, 130 million cell phones are thrown out, weighing approximately 65,000 tons. Recycling your old phone prevents hazardous elements like mercury, cadmium and lead from ending up in our landfills.

7. Offset Your Travel

If you or your loved ones are traveling more than 100 miles this holiday season, try to reduce air travel whenever possible. Also, consider offsetting the fossil fuel pollution generated by your trip, no matter how you travel.

These companies can help you get trees planted to reduce your impact.

- **Terrapass.com** - Provides carbon offsets for flying, driving, etc.

- **CarbonFund.org** - Provides a variety of carbon offset projects to choose from.

- **Carbonify.com** - Tree planting for offsetting carbon emissions.

8. Donate Your Time or Money to an Environmental Group

Get into the holiday spirit by volunteering! There are countless ways to help improve your community—and the planet—from cleaning up a local river to helping inner city kids experience the outdoors for the first time.

Organizations and charities all over the country need your time and/or your money to make a difference, so you can have a great impact for a small amount of effort.

9. Make DIY Gifts

There are so many ways to reduce your consumption impact when giving holiday gifts.

DIY gifts like homemade ornaments, crafty picture frames with photos of loved ones in them, homemade vanilla extract, or handmade beauty products can be as much fun to make and give as to receive.

There are tons of ideas on Pinterest, and you are really only limited by your imagination.

10. Give Experiential Gifts

My favorite gift to give is the gift of an experience. By giving gifts that can be experienced, like tickets to a baseball game, a trip somewhere interesting, or a homemade dinner, you can minimize wrapping and shopping, and still win points with the receiver.

Anything that allows your loved one to spend quality time experiencing something fun, new or interesting will make a gift sure to be remembered for years to come.

11. Purchase Eco-Friendly Presents

Finally, if you choose to purchase retail gifts, try to select products that come in minimal packaging, are made from sustainable materials, and can be easily recycled.

You could also choose gifts that help people live more sustainably, like a compost bin, a reusable water bottle, or a Wonderbag electricity-free slow cooker.

12. Stuff Your Stockings With Yummy, Natural Treats

Stocking stuffers tend to be small, plastic trinkets that end up in the garbage by the end of December.

Instead, fill your stockings with yummy, healthy treats like dried fruit, nuts, clementines and even homemade holiday cookies.

Whatever winter holiday you celebrate, there are many ways to make it green, frugal and bright!

Notes

1. http://www.epa.gov/region9/waste/recycling/index.html

2. Why locally sourced food is important - http://www.smallfootprintfamily.com/why-we-should-all-eat-locally/

3. Find an organic Christmas tree - http://www.greenpromise.com/resources/organic-christmas-trees.php

4.   Find a place to recycle your Christmas tree - http://
     www.realchristmastrees.org/dnn/AllAboutTrees/
     HowtoRecycle.aspx

What's Next?

Thank you for reading *Sustainability Starts at Home.*

I sincerely hope you enjoyed what you read in this book, and that it inspires you to take action today to make a difference for this lovely little planet we call home.

And speaking of making a difference, *there is one more easy way you can make a difference today...*

If you would be so kind, **please take a moment to leave a review of this book on Amazon.**

You see, the more reviews the book receives, the more Amazon will promote it to other people. This, in turn, really helps spread the word and puts this valuable information into more hands, so even more people can begin saving money while saving the planet, too.

Imagine what the world might be like if even just 5% of us were taking the steps in this book?

Your review can help make that happen, one book at a time.

So go leave a review now, before you get busy doing other things...

Thank you! I really appreciate it!

I also invite you to check out my website, **SmallFootprintFamily.com**, check out my **Sustainability Shop**, and subscribe to get hundreds more tips, recipes and inspirational articles for living a healthier, greener life— straight to your inbox!

Wishing you abundance, health and prosperity!

— Dawn

About the Author

Dawn Gifford is a work-at-home mom to a spirited 7 year-old girl, but before she became a mom, she was a Master Gardener and Master Composter, horticulture teacher and Cooperative Extension agent, as well as a certified arborist and Permaculture designer.

She founded one of the first greenroof companies and social enterprises in the nation (D.C. Greenworks), and spent most of the last 15 years developing award-winning workforce training programs for "green-collar" environmental jobs in tree care, greenroofing and bioretention, and urban agriculture.

Her "triple bottom line" company was sponsored by the USDA, the EPA, the D.C., Virginia and Maryland governments, the Ford Foundation, the Aspen Institute, and more, and was featured in *The Washington Post*, American Gardener magazine, the Washington Business Journal, and other publications.

Turning her interests to home and hearth after becoming a mother, she created **Small Footprint Family** to share her experience in sustainable living with a wider audience.

Dawn writes articles and books about:

- saving money while conserving water, energy, oil, trees and other natural resources;

- whole food nutrition and eco-friendly food choices (including tons of grain-free and dairy-free recipes);

- DIY and sustainable family living;

- non-toxic homes and natural healthcare; and

- gardening, homesteading and permaculture.

The aim of this book (and the mission of Small Footprint Family) is to give you the resources you need to make powerful choices that improve your health and well-being— and thereby the health and well-being of the only planet we've been blessed with.

Visit the site at www.smallfootprintfamily.com

Made in the USA
Las Vegas, NV
29 November 2022

60635892R00190